I0483392

FIGURING OUT THE FIGURINES
OF THE ANCIENT NEAR EAST

Edited by Stephanie M. Langin-Hooper

Occasional Papers in Coroplastic Studies 1, 2014
Association for Coroplastic Studies

COPYRIGHT © BY THE ASSOCIATION FOR COROPLASTIC STUDIES, 2014
All rights reserved
Published in the United States of America by
The Association for Coroplastic Studies

Manufactured in the United States of America

Library of Congress Cataloguing-in-Publication Data

Figuring Out the Figurines of the Ancient Near East / edited by Stephanie M. Langin-Hooper
Occasional Papers in Coroplastic Studies 1 / series editor, Jaimee P. Uhlenbrock

Includes bibliographical references.
ISBN: 978-0-9915533-1-0
1. Terra-cotta figurines–Israel.   2. Terra-cotta figurines–Jordan.   3. Terra-cotta figurines–Iraq.
4. Terra-cotta figurines–Syria.   Iraq–Antiquities.   6. Israel–Antiquities.   7. Jordan–Antiquities.
8. Syria–Antiquities.
9. Excavations (Archaeology)–Middle East–Congresses.   10. Near East–Antiquities–Congresses.
11. Near East--Civilization–To 622–Congresses.   12. Langin-Hooper, Stephanie M.

Printed on demand in the United States of America
by Lulu.com
www.Lulu.com

PREFACE

The series *Occasional Papers in Coroplastic Studies* came to fruition in order to promote the study of sculptural objects made in clay from the ancient Mediterranean and to facilitate their publication. An initiative of the Association for Coroplastic Studies (ACoST), formerly the Coroplastic Studies Interest Group (CSIG) of the Archaeological Institute of America, *Occasional Papers in Coroplastic Studies* is the first peer-reviewed publication venture of ACoST. This initial volume comprises 4 papers that were delivered at one of the three sessions of the Annual Meeting of the American Schools of Oriental Research (ASOR) either in 2009, 2010, or 2011 that were entitled "Figuring Out the Figurines of the Ancient Near East." I would like to thank Stephanie Langin-Hooper, who had organized these sessions, for also accepting the role of editor for this volume, which involved considerable time and energy on her part. I also would like to express my gratitude to the two anonymous reviewers of the papers that were submitted for this volume. Their valuable insights and direction were very much appreciated by the authors. Finally, I would like to thank the authors themselves for being so steadfast in their devotion to this project.

Jaimee P. Uhlenbrock
President, Association for Coroplastic Studies
February, 2014

Contents

GENERAL BIBLIOGRAPHY

4th International Congress
Proceedings of the 4th International Congress on the Archaeology of the Ancient Near East, (Berlin, 29 March–3 April 2004) Freie Universität Berlin. Volume 1: *The Reconstruction of Environment: Natural Resources and Human Interrelations through Time; Art History: Visual Communication,* H. Kühne et al (eds.), Wiesbaden: Harrassowitz Verlag.

Barrelet 1968
Barrelet, M.-T., *Figurines et reliefs en terre cuite de la Mésopotamie antique 1: Potiers, termes de métier, procédé de fabrication et production.* Bibliotèque Archéologique et Historique 85. Paris: Librairie Orientaliste Paul Geuthner.

Bilder als Quellen
Bilder als Quellen/Images as Sources: Studies on Ancient Near Eastern Artifacts and the Bible Inspired by the Work of Othmar Keel, S. Bickel et al (eds.), Orbis Biblicus et Orientalis Special Volume. Fribourg: Academic Press. Göttingen: Vendenhoeck & Ruprecht.

Daviau 2001
Daviau, P. M. M., "New Light on Iron Age Religious Iconography: The Evidence from Moab," *Studies in the History and Archaeology of Jordan* 7, pp. 317–326.

Images as Media
Images as Media: Sources for the Cultural History of the Near East and the Eastern Mediterranean (1st Millennium B.C.), C. Uehlinger (ed.), Orbis Biblicus et Orientalis 175, Fribourg: University Press. Göttingen: Vandenhoeck & Ruprecht

Kletter 1996
Kletter, R., *The Judean Pillar-Figurines and the Archaeology of Asherah,* British Archaeological Reports 636. Oxford: Tempus Reparatum.

van Buren 1930
Van Buren, E. D., *Clay Figurines of Babylonia and Assyria,* Yale Oriental Series 16, New Haven: Yale University Press.

Waraksa 2009
Waraksa, E. A., *Female Figurines from the Mut Precinct: Context and Ritual Function,* Orbis Biblicus et Orientalis 240, Fribourg: Academic Press; Goettingen: Vandenhoeck & Ruprecht.

FIGURING OUT THE FIGURINES OF THE ANCIENT NEAR EAST AT ASOR 2009-2011
Stephanie M. Langin-Hooper

Of all the objects produced by the cultures of the ancient Near East, figurines (particularly, although not exclusively, terracotta figurines) are among the most pervasive. For instance, over eleven-thousand figurine fragments were excavated from the Babylonian site of Seleucia-on-the-Tigris[1]—and such ubiquity is by no means unique to that city. Although when evaluated by modern aesthetic standards, figurines rarely rise to the artistic level of "great" monuments or statuary, they nevertheless seem to have had their own particular appeal, as well as a wide audience, in the ancient world. The use of inexpensive material and relative ease of manufacture meant that terracotta figurines were available to most ancient Near Eastern people. Terracotta figurines thus have the potential to be particularly informative about everyday life in these societies.

Yet, the study of terracotta figurines is also beset with obstacles to interpretation. At the most basic level, there is an often-unexpressed disagreement about how best to regard terracotta figurines: are they artworks or archaeological artifacts? A case can be made in either direction. On the side of art is the fact that, although not always the case, some terracotta figurines (such as the famous Tanagra figurines of the Hellenistic Greek world) seem designed with aesthetics as a major, if not primary, consideration. Even terracotta figurines that are not especially visually appealing are still capable of evoking an art-like response in their viewers. Because of their representational properties as miniature versions of life-size things (usually human beings or animals), terracotta figurines would seem to have the non-utilitarian, visually-engaging properties of an artwork. This effect is especially heightened when a terracotta figurine is seen, and studied, in isolation. As a single object, a figurine's representative capacity to mimetically link to the outside world, yet also present that world through the shifted perspective of miniaturization,[2] comes to the fore. Selective representation, altered mimesis—these are (some of) the properties of art.

However, figurines are rarely excavated or studied as single objects. Terracotta figurines are usually seen by the hundreds (if not the thousands), and such over-

whelming numbers suggest modes of scholarly analysis that are more similar to those used for potsherds than marble statuary. In addition to their prevalence, terracotta figurines are also generally viewed by scholars as being relatively mundane, due to the inexpensive nature of the ceramic material, their mass-produced or homemade manufacture by and for the non-elite, and the evaluation that many terracotta figurines were made with no special attention to artistic quality. The combination of these factors is often seen to situate terracotta figurines more within the domain of archaeologists than art historians. Archaeological approaches to terracotta figurines have often focused on extensive cataloguing and discussions of figurines (usually by "type") in general statements that apply to object groups. Such methodologies assist archaeologists in dealing with large numbers of terracotta figurines in a practical, manageable way. Assessing terracotta figurines as groups, rather than as individual objects, can also yield information, such as patterns of use and change across time, in ways more effective than individual artistic analysis would be. Yet, such methodological approaches also invite generalizations that gloss over variation—a particular problem at sites and in periods with marked figurine diversity—and often fail to consider the visual features of figurines as anything more than typological markers.

Terracotta figurines can thus be somewhat intractable and enigmatic. Positioned on the divide between the disciplines of art history and archaeology, they remain alluring, yet out of the full interpretive sweep of either discipline. As a result, many approaches to the voluminous numbers of figurines recovered from excavations in the ancient Near East regard them simply as objects to be categorized based on motif (such as "standing female") and then left with little more that is said about them. Analysis is often sweepingly broad, and assessments of function (such as "temple votive") rarely delve into the complexities of the human behaviors and social structures that would coincide with such figurine use.

There have always been exceptions to this trend. Within the field of ancient Near Eastern terracotta figurine studies, notably innovative analyses have been conducted by Julia Asher-Greve (1998), Julia Assante (2002), and Zainab Bahrani (2000), in particular; and even some earlier scholars, such as Wilhelmenia Van Ingen (1939), went beyond the simple catalogue in their publications of terracotta figurines. Yet despite this notable precedent, it has been only very recently that ancient Near Eastern figurine studies has experienced a turn of the tide in terms of both the prevalence of research specifically engaged with terracotta figurines, as well as an expansion of the methodologies used to study these elusive objects. Many of these new studies attempt to overhaul, or even to reinvent, how figurines are analyzed. In my own observation, two trends in these new methodological approaches seem to be emerging: scientific and quantitative studies that analyze figurine manufacture, use-life, and deposition; and object agency and materiality-based studies that focus on the human engagement (usually visual and tactile) with figurines as objects. Although the adherents of either approach are not restricted by a single methodology, it is nevertheless useful to provide a general overview of each analytical development.

Scientific and quantitative studies of ancient Near Eastern terracotta figurines have particularly prospered in the last decades because of technological advancements that allow for such investigations as the geological sourcing of clay, detecting of micro-fractures that can indicate deliberate breakage, computer models of figurine distribution on both localized and regional levels, and reconstructions of object circulation within social networks. The search for scientific facts that can be quantified, graphed, and otherwise inputted as "real" data has been seen by many as preferable to what are often regarded today as the more impressionistic analyses of figurines that took place in the 19th and 20th centuries. Even when studying figurines as archaeological artifacts, early cataloguing efforts that attempted to categorize often-illusive figurine motifs into clear sets of defined differences were based on a certain amount of connoisseurship. Analyses of figurine use were similarly rife with intuitive assumptions, often resulting in speculation about the role of figurines in society (usually as deities or votives) superseding, and even displacing, archaeological evidence for the figurines' use context. New quantitative approaches usually begin with the archaeology, rather than the object itself, and reconstruct figurine use and meaning based on detailed studies of contextual data. Studies of figurines as objects focus on quantifiable attributes, such as the texture of the clay or the length of the figurine's arms, rather than on the more nebulous aspects of figurine appearance, such as motifs, iconography, and style. Such approaches are often described as an attempt to introduce methodological rigor, which is already well-established in other archaeological studies (particularly of ceramics), into a field that has been the more traditional domain of qualitative analysis.

The other approach to terracotta figurine analysis that has been gaining traction within recent years is based on anthropological investigations of object agency and materiality. As with the quantitative analyses, studies of human-object engagement with terracotta figurines generally exhibit a macro-level interest in the role of terracotta figurines within a society and community. But rather than utilize standard archaeological explanations for figurine use (as votives or toys) and appearance (representations of deities or offerings), the object agency approach to figurine use asks why figurines, as miniature representations of large-scale living beings, objects, or structures, are appealing and have meaning within ancient societies. Douglass Bailey (2005) has been the pioneer of this avenue of terracotta figurine research. His work has revealed that figurines as miniature versions of life-size objects, particularly those of humans or animals, have an intimate and powerful quality. As Griselda Pollock has put it: "why do we like looking at images of other human beings? ... An image of another or even ourselves might have no meaning or actually threaten us. There must be a reason for and a mechanism by which we delight in images, especially those that are 'like' us, human images."[3] This power to enchant and engage—a power that all human images share—is intensified in figurines because of their miniature size. Miniature human images can be not only viewed, but they can also be possessed, in a complete physical sense. Such intimate relationships enable reciprocal identity sharing and transfer between person and figurine.[4] As I have argued in my own research, this particular power of figurines to display, as well as reshape, human identity means that they are an especially useful tool for archaeologists interested in accessing social roles, traditions, and interactions in the ancient world.[5] Object agency and materiality approaches to the study of terracotta figurines are endeavoring to pursue such social analysis, while also maintaining a focus on the individual figurine as a locus for meaningful interaction.

Together, these two new schools of terracotta figurine studies seem poised to remake scholarship's traditional understanding of terracotta figurines in the ancient Near East, and their connection to the societies who made and used them. Theoretical advancements in other fields, such as Mesoamerican and Neolithic European figurine studies, as well as technological developments in broader archaeological practice, have fueled the development of both approaches. But their application to ancient Near Eastern corpora, and the further expansion of these theories to suit the distinctive features of the ancient Near Eastern past, have been recent developments. It therefore seemed timely introduce a session specifically tailored to figurine studies at the Annual Meeting of the American Schools of Oriental Research.

This session, begun in 2009 and entitled "Figuring Out the Figurines of the Ancient Near East," aimed to bring together scholars researching terracotta figurines across all regions, sites and time periods in the ancient Near East, Egypt, and eastern Mediterranean. Prior to this session, papers on the topic of terracotta figurines were often presented at ASOR; however, they were always distributed across the conference, as they were slotted into sessions about regional specialties, such as the archaeology of Cyprus, or topics such as religion. This distribution of figurine papers across multiple sessions often did not allow for group discussion between figurine scholars. The "Figuring Out the Figurines" session aimed to provide a forum for idea presentation and discussion among a group of scholars who specialize in researching terracotta figurines. When the session was initially proposed, it was hoped that several benefits would result: encouraging interdisciplinary dialogue and cross-cultural comparisons of figurines; facilitating theoretical discussion about figurine interpretation; and fostering a sense of community among ancient Near East figurine scholars.

The response to the session was overwhelming. So many scholars submitted abstracts the first year that the session had to be given two time slots. The following two years also saw full slates of speakers, with deserving abstracts being turned away in the selection process. The audience response was equally enthusiastic. All three years saw audiences of 75-100 people, substantial crowds that far exceeded the average attendance at an ASOR session. Lively, informed discussion was frequent, both during the question-and-answer sessions and after the session concluded.

Based on these responses of both presenters and audiences, I judge the three-year run of "Figuring Out the Figurines of the Ancient Near East" to have been a success. Through this effort, the visibility of ancient Near Eastern figurine studies has been raised, and a community of scholars working in the field has become further interconnected. Although this incarnation of the "Figuring Out the Figurines" session has run its course at the ASOR Annual Meetings, it is my hope that figurine studies continue to be featured prominently at the conference, and that a revival of the session (at ASOR or another conference) might take place at some point in the future. As figurine studies continue to advance through new archaeological discoveries, new theoretical breakthroughs, and innovative approaches to figurine interpretation, the need for an ancient Near East figurine conference forum will continue. It is crucial that all scholars concerned with the study of these intriguing objects remain connected in productive collaboration and mutual idea-sharing, to further the efforts of our unique discipline.

ASOR CONFERENCE PROGRAMS OF THE "FIGURING OUT THE FIGURINES SESSIONS," 2009-2011

Before proceeding to the introduction of the papers in this volume, I would first like to acknowledge the ASOR staff and organizing committee for their strong support of this project. Additionally, all of the scholars who participated in the three years of "Figuring Out the Figurines"—as speakers, facilitators, audience members, or supporters—have my sincere thanks. The session chairs, speakers, and paper titles are listed here:

ASOR 2009 (New Orleans), Session 1

STEPHANIE M. LANGIN-HOOPER (University of California, Berkeley), Presiding

ADI ERLICH (University of Haifa),"Double Faces, Multiple Meanings: the Hellenistic Pillar Figurines from Maresha, Israel"

ERIN WALCEK AVERETT (Creighton University), "The Ritual Contexts of Archaic Cypriote Figurines"

JAIMEE P. UHLENBROCK (SUNY New Paltz), "A Near Easterner at Cyrene: Cross-Cultural Implications at a Greek City in Libya"

ERIN D. DARBY (Duke University) and DAVID BEN-SHLOMO (Hebrew University, Jerusalem), "Sugar and Spice and Everything Nice: Terracotta Pillar Figurines

and Jerusalemite Pottery Production in Iron II Judea"
Susan Downey (University of California, Los Angeles), "Images of Divinities in Terracotta and Stucco Plaques from the Hellenistic-Roman Period at Dura-Europos, Syria"

ASOR 2009 (New Orleans), Session 2
Andrea Creel (University of California, Berkeley), Presiding
Christopher Tuttle (American Center of Oriental Research, Jordan), "The Nabataean Coroplastic Arts: A Synthetic Methodology for Addressing a Diverse Corpus"
Elizabeth Waraksa (University of California, Los Angeles), "Female Figurines from the Mut Precinct, Karnak: Evidence of Ritual Use"
Elizabeth Bloch-Smith (St. Joseph's University), "Nudity is Divine: Southern Levantine Female Figurines"

ASOR 2010 (Atlanta)
Stephanie M. Langin-Hooper (University of California, Berkeley), Presiding
Rüdiger Schmitt (University of Muenster), "Animal Figurines as Ritual Media in Ancient Israel"
Christopher Tuttle (American Center of Oriental Research, Jordan), "Nabataean Camels & Horses in Daily Life: The Coroplastic Evidence"
Erin Darby (Duke University), "Seeing Double: Viewing and Re-viewing Judean Pillar Figurines through Modern Eyes"
Adi Erlich (University of Haifa), "The Emergence of Enthroned Females in Hellenistic Terracottas from Israel: Cyprus, Asia Minor, and Canaanite Connections"
P. M. Michèle Daviau (Wilfrid Laurier University), "The Coroplastic Traditions of Transjordan"
Rick Hauser (International Institute for Mesopotamian Area Studies), "Reading Figurines: Animal Representations in Terra Cotta from Urkesh, the first Hurrian Capital (2450 BCE)"

ASOR 2011 (San Francisco)
Stephanie M. Langin-Hooper (Bowling Green State University), Presiding
Rüdiger Schmitt (University of Muenster), "Apotropaic Animal Figurines"
Marco Ramazzotti (La Sapienza University of Rome), "The Mimesis of a World: The Early Bronze and Middle

Bronze Clay Figurines from Ebla-Tell Mardikh (Syria)"
Doug Bailey (San Francisco State University), "Uncertainty and Precarious Partiality: New Thinking on Figurines"
Christopher Tuttle (American Center of Oriental Research, Jordan), "Miniature Nabataean Coroplastic Vessels"
Erin Darby (University of Tennessee) and Michael Press (University of Arkansas), "Composite Figurines in the Iron II Levant: A Comparative Approach"
Andrea Creel (University of California, Berkeley), "Manipulating the Divine and Late Bronze/Iron Age 'Astarte' Plaques in the Southern Levant"

DISCUSSION OF PAPERS INCLUDED IN THIS VOLUME
All participants from the three-year run of the "Figuring Out the Figurines of the Ancient Near East" session at the 2009-2011 ASOR Annual Meetings were given the opportunity to submit articles for publication. The four peer-reviewed articles included in this issue are the result of that process. Fortuitously, they represent the breadth and diversity—both in temporal and geographical scope, as well as in theoretical approaches—that was exhibited over the three years of the ASOR session. Each can stand alone as a contribution to its respective field; however, together they represent the progress being made in figurine studies throughout ancient Near Eastern scholarship.

P. M. Michèle Daviau's contribution, "The Coroplastics of Transjordan: Forming Techniques and Iconographic Traditions in the Iron Age," is immediately notable in its treatment of the diversity of figurine forms found in Transjordan. Although difficult to classify, the unique or uncommon figurines in the corpus are nevertheless given equal treatment in this article with the more popular and easily categorized forms. Daviau powerfully demonstrates how classification of figurines can still be a useful tool without resorting to the over-generalizations and disregard for uncommon figurine forms that are so common to figurine typologies. In the analysis of her material, Daviau utilizes an object-experience methodology to address issues of use. Her assessment that many of the Transjordan figurines cannot stand alone, but must be held in the hand or propped up, is an excellent example of how object materiality can yield useful information about the function and experience of terracotta figurines. Daviau's detailed study of figurine manufacture and iconography, along with quantitative analysis of figurine distribution across several ancient sites, is also representative of the recent trend in figurine scholarship towards more scientific studies. Daviau thus combines both of the new approaches to figurine analysis in order to shed important light on the expression of ethnic identity in the terracotta figurines of Transjordan.

Erin Darby's contribution, "Seeing Double: Viewing and Re-viewing Judean Pillar Figurines through Modern Eyes," is strongly positioned within the quantitative approach to ancient Near Eastern figurines. Yet, uncharacteristically for a quantitative study, Darby's article investigates iconography and motifs traditionally seen as the domain of art historians. Darby catalogues individual elements of the figurines in her corpus in order to determine how artisans drew upon a broad repertoire of available symbols and recombined them to create specific visual forms and functions in the figurines. An important critique of the tradition of impressionistic studies of figurines in scholarship is made; particularly enlightening is the critique that viewing and looking at objects is culturally-situated and conditioned, so any correlation between modern and ancient ways of seeing must be demonstrated, not assumed. Darby's article is uncommon in that its discussion of terracotta figurine iconography is presented with few accompanying images, none of which illustrate the specific figurines presented in her article. This is a compelling, and innovative, way to oblige the reader to think about figurines from ancient perspectives, rather than jumping immediately to visual assessment based on modern cultural norms. The article's comparison of the terracotta figurines with other artifacts from the Judean culture to discover iconographical similarities outside the figurine corpus is also a significant step forward for the field, as archaeologists often focus on figurines as a special class of objects, obscuring their functional, display, and visual similarities to other forms of material culture.

Adi Erlich's contribution, "Double Face, Multiple Meanings: The Hellenistic Pillar Figurines from Maresha," utilizes both of the new approaches to terracotta figurine analysis. The article begins with quantitative assessment of figurine types and distribution across the landscape and sites near Maresha. From this scientific analysis, Erlich progresses to a detailed consideration of the human interaction with, and meanings created through the materiality of, terracotta figurines with two faces. Her article takes a theoretically-informed perspective on the fluidity of "meaning" as a product of the encounter between the person and the object, with the conclusion that terracotta figurines were interpreted differently, and took on different identities, based on the cultural background and particular interests of their viewer. In Erlich's view, the interaction between human and figurine was dynamic, and only partially determined by the physical appearance of the object. The relationship of figurine forms to broader social issues of cross-cultural interaction and ethnic difference are discussed in the conclusion of the article, in which it is suggested that the "double face" figurines were accessible to most members of the Maresha community during otherwise tumultuous times. Erlich's line of argumentation seems to suggest that these figurines participated in broader social processes in which ethnic and culture differences were minimized ——a powerful example of the role and agency of terracotta figurines within the communities who made and used them.

Marco Ramazzotti's contribution, "The Mimesis of a World: The Early and Middle Bronze Clay Figurines from Ebla-Tell Mardikh," is the most at home in the new branch of figurine theory that deals with anthropological approaches to materiality and investigates the intimate encounters between person and object that figurines encourage. Nevertheless, Ramazzotti also utilizes quantitative studies of figurine context and use at Ebla, as well as chemical and physical analysis of figurine breakage patterns, to support his argument. He thus demonstrates that both approaches to figurine analysis can be used together productively, especially to focus on the material presence and properties of a figurine, which have both a quantitative and a qualitative (human experience) component. The tactile element of human experience with figurines is especially highlighted in the article and used to explore how miniature clay versions of beings can substitute for (and allow experimentation with) the life-size, real social world. Ramazzotti's conclusion that the spatial distribution of figurines at Ebla, as well as the tactile experience of these diverse figurine forms, indicates that broader social issues beyond the sacred kingship were being addressed through terracotta figurines, is a striking example of the interpretive possibilities offered by both current approaches to figurine analysis. His discussion of creation versus mimesis, and the linkages of both concepts with Mesopotamian literary sources, is a valuable addition to theoretical discussions of Mesopotamian figurines.

Conclusion

The four articles presented in this volume provide an excellent cross-section, as well as some of the most compelling examples, of the approaches to terracotta figurines presented in the three years of the "Figuring Out the Figurines of the Ancient Near East" sessions at the American Schools of Oriental Research Annual Meetings. All four articles fit within at least one of the two current trends in figurine scholarship, and many of them suggest that these two approaches can be productively combined. I would suggest that this combination of rigorous quantitative studies of figurines-as-artifacts focusing on contextual and physical data, with the more theoretical approaches to figurine agency, materiality, and human-object interaction, will be the future of our field. It is my hope that future coference sessions, at at ASOR and elsewhere, will provide the valuable forums necessary for those of us engaged in terracotta figurine studies to continue to share our research and to enrich our community with with further innovations and methodological developments.

Acknowledgements

My primary thanks go to Jaimee Uhlenbrock, who first approached me about creating this volume and did most of the editing work (even though she generously insisted on giving me editorial attribution). Without her, this valuable project would never have come to fruition. I would also like to thank all four of the authors, as well as the two anonymous peer reviewers; without their cooperation and incredible patience this publication would not have succeeded.

This volume is based on research that was originally presented at the American Schools of Oriental Research Annual Meetings. I would like to thank ASOR for sponsoring the original conference sessions, and believing in my vision that "Figurine Studies" had a place in the annual meeting. Many thanks go to all of the presenters who gave insightful and innovative papers during the three years of the session, as well as to the audience members who came to hear the speakers and participate in the lively and informed discussion.

Notes

[1] Menegazzi 2012: 157

[2] The most immediate way in which figurines present a shifted perspective on the world is by their miniaturization. However, other changes to the life-size human/animal body, clothing, etc. are often made to terracotta figurines; such changes have the potential to further alter the way in which the figurine's viewer encounters the object, and the way in which the object can alter the viewer's perception of the world. Bailey 2005 is the ideal reference for further reading on the ways in which terracotta figurines and other miniature objects present alternate perspectives on, and experiences of, reality.

[3] Pollock 2003: 182

[4] Bailey 2005: 38

[5] Langin-Hooper 2013

Bibliography

Asher-Greve 1998	Asher-Greve, J. M. "The Essential Body: Mesopotamian Conceptions of the Gendered Body," in *Gender and the Body in the Ancient Mediterranean*, M. Wyke (ed.), Oxford and Malden, M.A.: Blackwell Publishers, pp. 8-37.
Assante 2002	Assante, J. "Style and Replication in 'Old Babylonian' Terracotta Plaques: Strategies for Entrapping the Power of Images," in *Ex Mesopotamia et Syria Lux, Festschrift fur Manfried Dietrich*, O. Loretz, K. Metzler, and H. Schaudig (eds.), Munster: Ugarit-Verlag, pp. 1-29.
Bahrani 2000	Bahrani, Z. *Women of Babylon: Gender and Representation in Mesopotamia*, London: Routledge.
Bailey 2005	Bailey, D. *Prehistoric Figurines: Representation and Corporeality in the Neolithic*, London and New York: Routledge.

Langin-Hooper 2013   Langin-Hooper, S. M. "Terracotta Figurines and Social Identities in Hellenistic Babylonia," in *Critical Approaches to Ancient Near Eastern Art*, M.H. Feldman and B. Brown (eds.), Berlin and Boston: De Gruyter, pp. 451-479.

Menegazzi 2012   Menegazzi, R. "Creating a new language: the terracotta figurines from Seleucia on the Tigris," in *Proceedings of the International Congress on the Archaeology of the Ancient Near East*, Band 7: Volume 2: *Ancient & Modern Issues in Cultural Heritage, Colour & Light in Architecture, Art & Material Culture, Islamic Archaeology*, R. Matthews and J. Curtis (eds.), Wiesbaden-Erbenheim: Harrassowitz Verlag, pp. 157–167.

Pollock 2003   Pollock, G. "The Visual," in *A Concise Companion to Feminist Theory*, M. Eagleton (ed.), Malden, MA: Blackwell Publishing, pp. 773-794.

Van Ingen 1939   Van Ingen, W. *Figurines from Seleucia on the Tigris: Discovered by the Expeditions Conducted by the University of Michigan with the Cooperation of the Toledo Museum of Art and the Cleveland Museum of Art 1927-1932*, Ann Arbor: The University of Michigan Press.

STEPHANIE M. LANGIN-HOOPER
Bowling Green State University
slangin@bgsu.edu

The Coroplastics of Transjordan
Forming Techniques and Iconographic Traditions in the Iron Age
P. M. Michèle Daviau[1]

Abstract

During the past twenty years, excavations in Transjordan have produced a large corpus of anthropomorphic figurines and statues, as well as figures attached to architectural models. For the most part, these figures originate in central Jordan and date to the Iron Age. Although they were found in tombs and at a limited number of sites, the figurines and statues in this study represent a variety of ethnic and cultural traditions, many previously unknown. While it is clear in certain instances that Egypto-Phoenician iconography had an influence on Ammonite and Moabite iconographic traditions, in other cases the imagery, especially of the ceramic statues, is distinctive and/or unique. This paper will present a discussion of the various forming techniques employed to produce these figures and begin to explore their place in the iconographic traditions of the region. Included in this study will be a review of figurines found previously and identified with confidence by early explorers and excavators as Ammonite, Moabite, or Edomite on the basis of the ceramic tradition represented in a given region. In view of the much larger corpus which is now available, considerable diversity in the assemblage is evident and a reassessment is warranted.

Area under Study

The central Jordanian plateau in the Iron Age included a number of small polities, some more centralized than others. Best known is Ammon, whose capital at Rabbath-Ammon (`Amman) retains vestiges of a royal citadel with impressive architecture and works of art. On Ammon's southwestern perimeter were the Land of Madaba and the plains of Moab, which supported organized tribal groups during Iron Age I–early Iron II.[2] On the plateau to the south, two distinct polities known as Moab and Edom developed during Iron Age II (900–600 BCE). Several major trade routes linking Arabia with Damascus passed through these regions, providing for the exchange of raw materials and cultural traditions.

Specific sites of interest on the plateau[3] that have yielded a significant number of Iron Age figurines include `Amman, Tall al-`Umayri, Tall Jawa, Khirbat al-Mudayna ath-Thamad, WT-13, Balu`a, and Busayra, with smaller numbers from Maqabalayn, Sahab, Hesban, Jalul, Madaba, Mount Nebo, Dibon, and Tawilan.[4] One hundred ninety-four figurines and

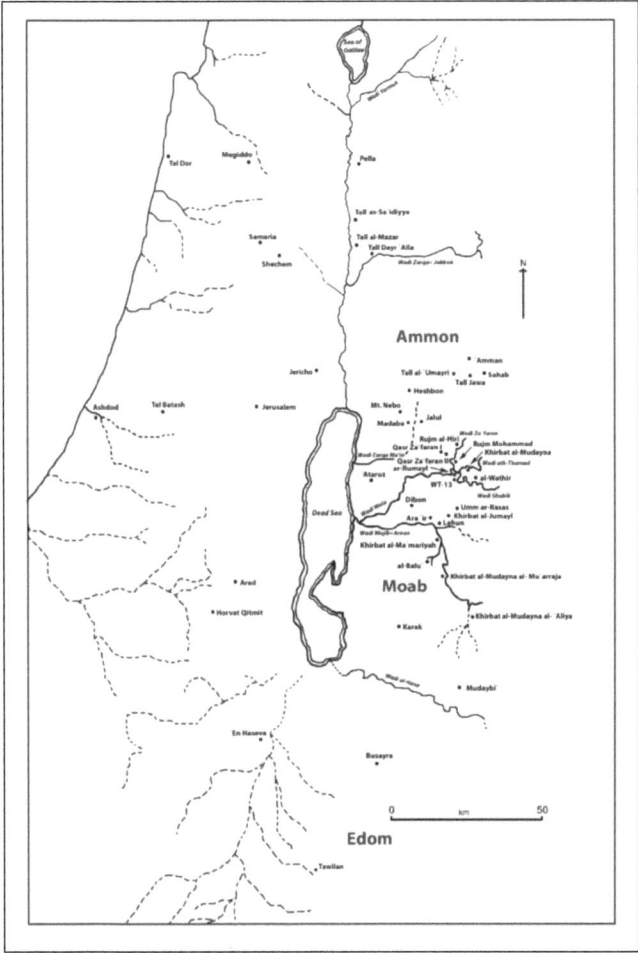

Fig. 1. Map of central Jordan and Palestine.

29 ceramic statues from published reports and from excavations in Moab under my direction are included in this study;[5] figurines with suspect provenience are not discussed in detail.

The anthropomorphic figures from central Jordan consist primarily of terracotta figurines and ceramic statues, with stone figures playing a minor role.[6] Terracotta figurines represent females and males as free-standing fully modeled figures, either mold-made or hand-made, and pillar figurines with mold-made heads. The smaller corpus of ceramic statues is, for the most part, pillar-shaped in style, with few details of the anatomy shown below the waist. Only

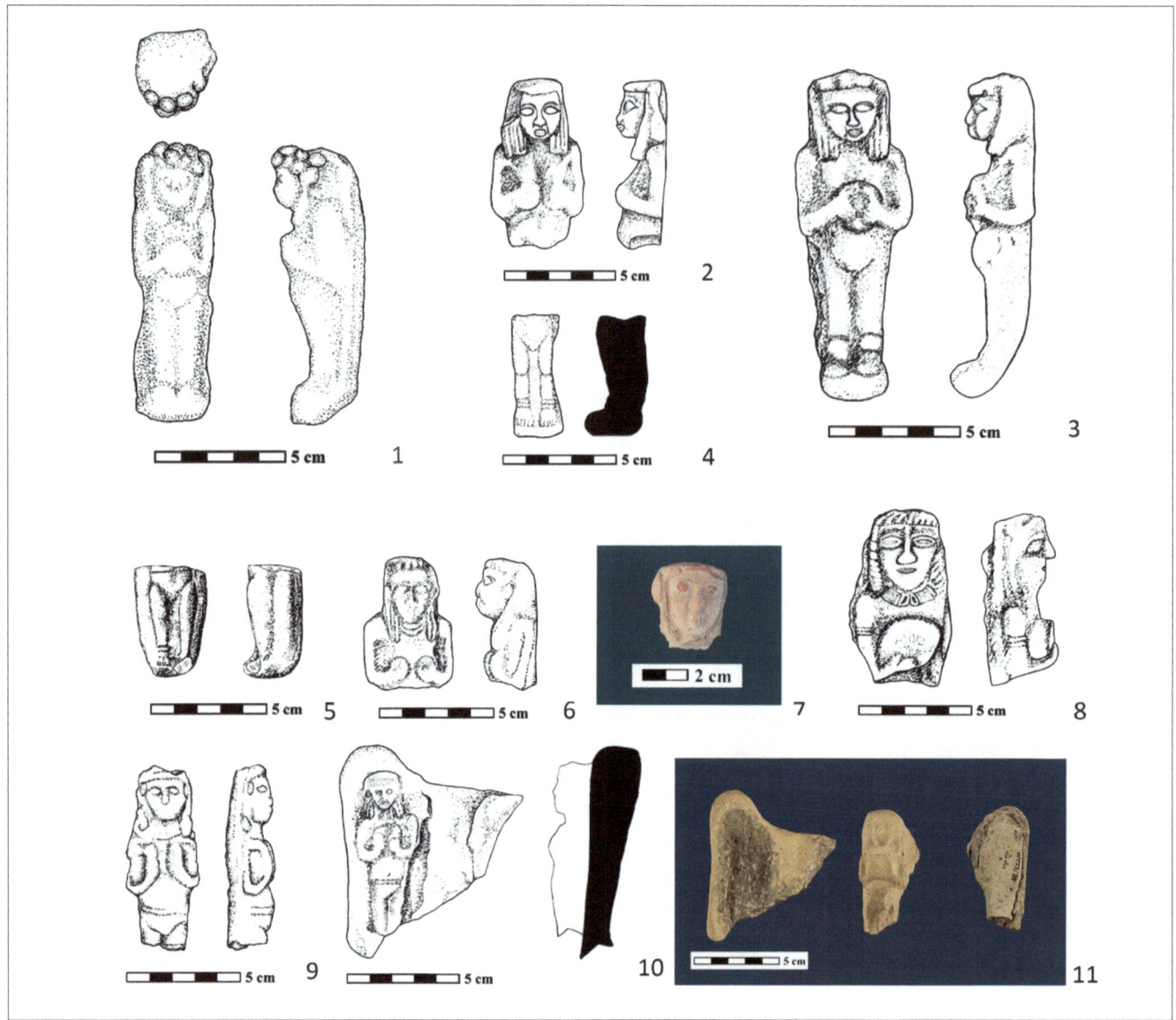

Fig. 2. Free-Standing and Attached Figurines; 1) finger formed (WT 21-1/521); 2) tool formed back (WT 35-2/535); 3) curved feet (WT 86-2/586); 4) flat base (WT 95-2/595); 5) excessive clay (TJ 1712; after Daviau 2002: fig. 2.30:3); 6-7) details of hair (WT 68-2/568; MT 565–4/21); 8-9) details of jewelry (WT 42-2/542; WT 286-4/514); 10–11) attached to a plaque or fronton (WT 88+89-2/588+589).

a handful of limestone statuettes have been recovered and these, along with the large stone statues from the `Amman area, are beyond the scope of this study.[7] So too are the large collections of zoomorphic figurines that deserve separate investigation.[8]

BASIC FIGURINE TYPES

Free-standing, mold-made figures:
Solid mold-made ceramic figurines were formed either in the round (bivalve mold) or, more often, were molded on the front (univalve) and trimmed on the back, either with the potter's finger or a tool. The result of trimming with one's finger is evident in the gently rounded back of those figurines which retain additional clay behind the body (WT 21-2/521, Fig. 2.1), whereas tool-trimmed figurines have a flattened back which in some cases truncated the arms and legs (WT 35-2/535, Fig. 2.2; WT 286-4/514; WT 77-2/577). Although solid figurines have a vertical stance, they cannot stand up alone since the feet are often positioned at an angle in order to fully depict the feet (WT 86-2/586, Fig. 2.3). Although these figurines were designed to be carried or to lean against another object,[9] in some instances there is a small flat support for the feet (WT 95-2/595, Fig. 2.4). All of these figurines are distinct from so–called 'plaque

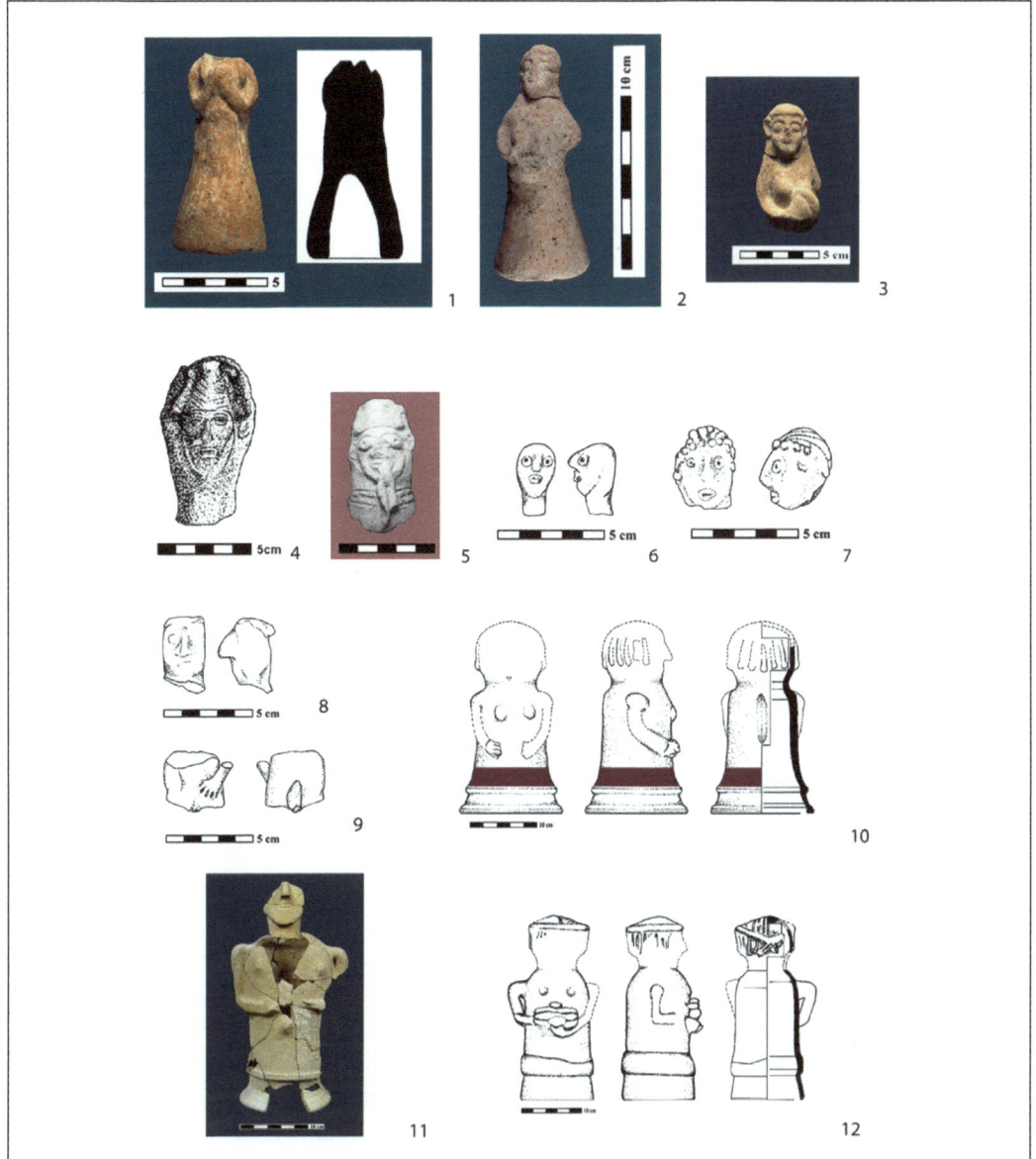

Fig. 3. Pillar figurines; 1) Wheel-made base (WT 72-2/572); 2) sloping shoulder (WT 479-6/526); 3) additional features (WT 53-2/553); 4) *atef* crown (TJ 100); 5) Jalul, used with permission); 6–9) male heads and bodies (WT 282-4/510, WT 466–6/505, WT 521-6/520, WT 323-5/508); 10-12) statues (WT 37-2/537, WT 11-1/511, WT 166-2/666).

figurines' which typically have a molded form impressed on a larger slab/plaque of clay that frames the figure on all sides. This Late Bronze–Iron I style is rare in central Jordan; for example, one figurine from late Iron Age II Tall Jawa in Ammon consists of the lower body of a female pressed against a thicker clay backing (TJ 1712, Fig. 2:5).[10] Even in this example, the backing is rounded, closer to the hand-finished style seen on figurines from WT-13 than to the flat slab or plaque of earlier figurines. Plaque figurines are found in Late Bronze Age II contexts at various sites, such as Tell Beit Mirsim,[11] Megiddo,[12]

Tel eṣ-Ṣafi/Gath[13] and, in smaller numbers, at Tall al-ʿUmayri,[14] and Lahav.[15]

After the figurine was removed from the mold, additional attention to detail was completed, such as incised lines representing strands of hair (WT 68; WT 86-2/568, Fig. 2:6; WT 518) or the addition of pellets to represent curls (WT 21-2/521, Fig. 2.1; WT 466-6/505, Fig. 3:7), a feature that applies to both female and male figurines. Paint was used on occasion to highlight features such as hair and eyebrows (MT 565-4/21, Fig. 2.7); in other instances, it is apparent that paint covered the entire figurine although in their current condition, the paint is only preserved in grooves and depressions in the surface. Necklaces, bracelets, armbands (WT 42-2/542; Fig. 2.8) and anklets (WT 95-2/595; Fig. 2.4) are also shown, although it is not clear in all cases whether these details were added by hand or were already present in the mold itself. Along with their jewelry, the line of the girdle on the abdomen and details of the anatomy (MT 566-4/22; WT 286-4/514, Fig. 2:9) are sometimes shown and/or enhanced on naked female figures. Facial features such as eyes, nose and mouth were partially designed in the mold and later enhanced by hand;[16] in a few instances, a small pellet was added to enlarge the eye and the pupil was either painted (MT 565-4/21, Fig. 2.7) or punctated (for example, Jalul, WT 282-4/510, 466-6/505, Fig. 3:5-7).

Free-standing figurines could also be attached to another object, such as an architectural model or ceramic stand. This can be done in a number of ways; the figure may be pressed onto another object[17] or attached with the addition of clay packed around all sides to seal it to the object (WT 88+89-2/588+589, Fig. 2:10, 11) or, thirdly, the figure could be attached only along one side (WT 86-2/586, Fig. 2:3). Figures that were attached on all sides were clearly made as free-standing figurines before a coil of clay was added as a seal. A small number of hand-made attached figurines represent a different technique; these were formed as integrated components of an architectural model (WT 80-2/580, WT 179-2/679) and protrude from one side or edge of the miniature structure.

Pillar Figurines:
Pillar figurines have a conical base, a mold-made head, and attached arms and breasts. The pillar was formed either by hand with a concave base[18] or made on the wheel, a practice evident from the rills on the interior of the lower body (WT 72-2/572, Fig. 3:1). The cone was then cut from the hump and inverted and a depression was made in the top of the pillar to receive the tenon extending from the neck. The mold-made head and neck ends in a peg-shaped tenon that was inserted into the top of the pillar. Extra clay was then added to secure the head to the pillar and form the shoulders. This extra clay was often poorly molded with the result that the shoulders sloped down onto the body (WT 190-4/501; WT 479-6/526, Fig. 3:2). In contrast to the standardization of the mold-made pillar figurine heads found in Judah[19] and represented at Tel `Aroer,[20] the facial features of pillar figurines from Transjordan are considerably more varied, with some figurines having pronounced eyebrows, large eyes, chins and ears,[21] while others have delicate features (WT 315-5/505) and an elaborate hair style, such as the drum player from Tomb 84 at Mount Nebo.[22] Hand-made additions to the pillar figurine may include small coils of clay to fashion the arms, pellets for breasts, mittens for hands and a clay disc to represent a frame drum (WT 53-2/553, Fig. 3:3). In one case, a Judean-style molded head found at Khirbat al-Mudayna ath-Thamad was enhanced by the addition of small coils of clay framing her face to form curls in the style of the Egyptian goddess Hathor. A second style, seen at Balu` and at WT-13, is the veiled female figure that appears either as a pillar figurine or as an attached figure.[23]

Due to poor preservation, many figurines are represented only by their head. While it is apparent that molds were used to form many of these heads, there is great variety in facial features. The lack of repetition makes it difficult to assign an exact identification or function for many of the female figures. The differences in hair style and the presence of veiled female figures in cultic and domestic contexts in both northern and central Moab add to this uncertainty.

Partially preserved figurines:
Identification and determination of function is also difficult for the male heads and crudely-made heads of figures with indeterminate gender. Complete male figures are rare but a wide variety of head styles make their appearance. Best known are mold-made heads wearing an *atef* crown or conical cap, a style that continues into the Persian period in the Levant. These are typically slipped or painted to show the beard and/or mustache, such as a complete figurine from a tomb at Maqabalayn[24] and a head from the `Amman citadel,[25] while the paint on a male head from Tall Jawa is faded (TJ 100, Fig. 3:4). A double flute player with *atef* crown from Jalul also appears mold-made (Fig. 3:5). This figurine has depressed pupils which may have been added by hand (Fig. 3.2), as was the case for two male heads from WT-13—these males are shown either bald (WT 282-4/510, Fig. 3:6) or with curls (WT 466-6/505, Fig. 3:7). The most elaborate head has long locks of hair held in place with a headband.[26] Male heads with a conical headdress are found at `Amman[27] and Tall al-`Umayri.[28] In contrast to these carefully formed heads, hand-made male heads that are stylized

appear with only the nose and cap clearly formed (WT 521-6/520, Fig. 3:8). One body fragment from WT-13 suggests that some male figures were shown nude (WT 323-5/508, Fig. 3:9), as is a limestone statue from Khirbat al-Mudayna ath-Thamad (MT 2974) and a small, silt stone figure from Tall Jawa.[29]

Unique Figurine Types:
A small number of hand-made torso fragments are unique, such as the small figure seated on a throne or architectural model fragment (WT 472-6/506) and a second seated figure, somewhat larger in size and missing its head and limbs (WT 439-6/501).[30] Most distinctive among the hand-made figurines is a pair of legs, each made separately and then pressed together (WT 13a+b-1/513). The position of these feet is similar to certain mold-made figurines in that they are not flat on the bottom, although a single foot and lower leg (WT 110-2/610) and the feet and legs of a naked female (WT 95-2/595) are flat enough to stand on their own.

A naked female molded onto the side of a hand-made pillar[31] is distinct from other pillar figurines mentioned above. So too is a mold-made female figure, also from Tall Jawa, that appears to be seated on a winged chair; this figure has as its best parallels figurines from Aegean sites such as Tanagra, Locris, and Corinth.[32]

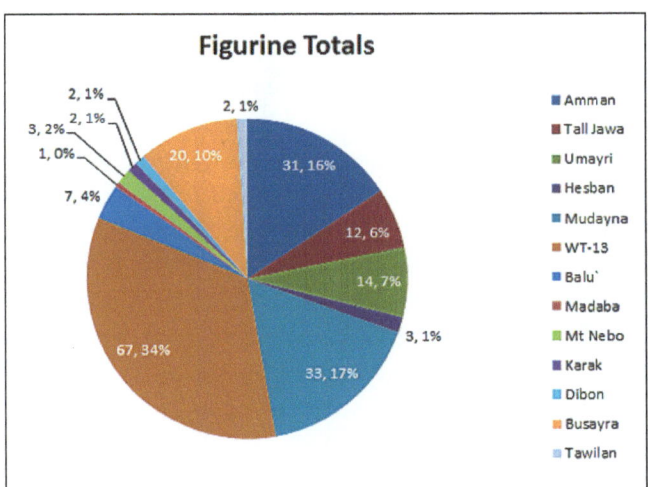

Chart 1. Distribution of Figurines in Central and Southern Jordan

DISTRIBUTION AND QUANTIFICATION
When we quantify the figurines from sites in central Jordan (Chart 1, Figurine Totals), the largest concentrations known to this writer come from `Amman, Khirbat al-Mudayna ath-Thamad, WT-13 and Busayra[33]

with nearly equal representation from Tall Jawa and Tall al-`Umayri.[34] Smaller numbers come from excavations at Hesban, Balu`a, Madaba, Mount Nebo, Karak, Dibon and Tawilan,[35] with isolated examples from Jalul and Maqabalayn.[36]

The second important class of ceramic figures consists of statues. Fragments and body sherds of statues are often not recognized as such or are classified as figurines, while hollow heads are identified as, or confused with, masks. I have classified small hollow figures as statues based on their similarity to the 20 statues of various sizes recovered at WT-13 and known from sites in Israel.[37] The statues were made on the wheel with the base fashioned in the same manner as the rim and neck of a jug or storejar (WT 37-2/537, Fig. 3:10). Clear evidence of rills and tool marks on the interior indicate this process, while the locks of hair, ears and other features were hand-made. The breasts were either formed separately and attached or were formed by pushing out the wall of the body. The heads were probably formed separately and then attached, since many statues are broken at the point of attachment (WT 11-1/511, Fig. 3:11). Two of the statues from Busayra have lamps on their head and one holds a disc parallel to the body[38] in the same position as many of the WT-13 figurines.

The arms of these statues were made from a clay coil, like a loop handle, and were pressed against the torso for support. The largest statue (WT 11-2/511) was painted with horizontal bands—only in a few places is there evidence for faded vertical stripes, while other statues retain a horizontal band of color on the lower body (Fig. 3:10). One figure holds several small loaves, each made separately and then pressed together (WT 166-2/666, Fig. 3:12). This same figure has attached locks of hair with a clear part in the middle and a hair band around his head which is knotted in the back. This hair style appears on several other statue heads, one of which supports a lamp attached above a headband which is decorated with pellets (WT 98-2/598). Other hand-made features include pellets for eyes, ears with holes for earrings, and noses, both simple and elegant in form. Quantification of statues (Chart 2, Statue Totals) yields only two concentrations, WT-13 and the Busayra area, with isolated examples from Tall Jawa, Tall Madaba,[39] Tall Damiya in the Jordan Valley[40] and Ṣabkhah in northern Jordan,[41] reflecting the small number of Iron Age sites excavated and published to date.

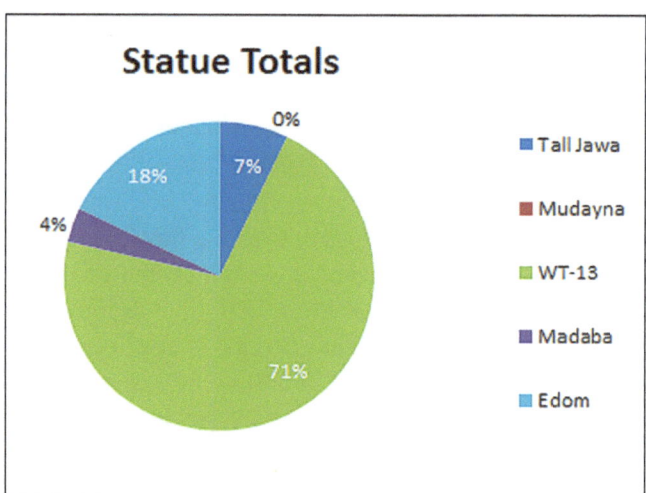

Statue Totals

- Tall Jawa
- Mudayna
- WT-13
- Madaba
- Edom

0%
7%
18%
4%
71%

Chart 2. Distribution of Ceramic Statues in Central and Southern Jordan

ORIGIN OF THE CERAMIC FIGURES

The diversity of styles among the figures in this study and the recognition of various clay matrices with few links with figures from neighboring sites lead to the supposition that the figurines and statues at WT-13 were not all local products. In order to test this hypothesis, 10 samples from WT-13 and one from Mudayna ath-Thamad were submitted for NAA analysis to Jan Gunneweg and Marta Balla at Budapest for comparison with similar statues from Ḥorvat Qitmit and ʿEn Ḥaṣeva.[42] By comparison of their results with databases that include Judah and Edom, it was clear that only one sample from WT-13 and one from Mudayna Thamad were similar to a lamp from ʿEn Ḥaṣeva, while another sample had parallels at Busayra and ʿEn Ḥaṣeva.[43] The remaining Moabite samples fell into two groups, neither of which has parallels known at this time. Figurines from Ammon have not yet been tested by NAA.

MOTIFS

Due to the fragmentary nature of many of the figures from Transjordan, the iconographic details are often lacking. As a result, the understanding of the iconographic traditions of Transjordan is in its infancy. Nevertheless, there are three motifs that appear dominant: figurines and small statues holding a disc at the waist,[44] female figurines playing a drum, and females holding their breasts. Other musical instruments are also attested: a male flute player from Jalul[45] and a lyre player from ʿAmman.[46] Only 4 figures obviously have their arms at their sides, while several statues have their hands on their abdomen or hold a bowl, a lamp, a stack of bread loaves, or an animal in their arms, positions that suggest that these ceramic figures were votive representations of worshipers.[47] The same is probably the case for those statues with a lamp on their head. Recognizable deity figures are few and are better known among stone statues from Rabbath-Ammon and among the small *atef*-crowned male heads. The precise function of naked female figures that hold their breasts or cover them with their hands, comparable in style to figurines from Megiddo[48] and Cyprus,[49] remains unclear, although they may represent Astarte or Anat.[50] These are, however, very different in style from the Judean pillar figurines with larger breasts[51] most probably related to the goddess Asherah and which may be symbolic of lactation.[52] Female heads with ornate earrings and necklaces from Tall Jawa[53] and in a mold from ʿAmman[54] have parallels to the 'woman at the window' depicted on Phoenician ivory inlays, whose precise meaning is in doubt.

Apart from the male figures with an *atef* crown or conical headdress, each male figurine is unique and its association with a specific iconographic tradition cannot be determined at present. The same is true of the small seated figures. However, the statues, both male and female, are part of a much larger tradition. They have their best parallels at Ḥorvat Qitmit and ʿEn Ḥaṣeva[55] and in the extensive repertoire from Phoenician sites across the Mediterranean, especially at Bithia.[56]

Ethnic differences can best be seen in the variation in hair styles[57] and head coverings for both male and female figures. Among the statues, the dominant style shows individual locks held in place with a headband; this style is in contrast to male figurines that appear bald, with curls, or with a crown or hat. At present, the small numbers involved makes it difficult to interpret certain of these styles satisfactorily. Nevertheless, the recovery of an increasing number of ceramic figurines from current excavations and their ongoing publication is rapidly expanding the repertoire from central Jordan. As a result, future research should make it possible to better understand the forming techniques and unique styles of the coroplastic traditions of Transjordan.

NOTES

[1] Director of the Wadi ath-Thamad Project, Jordan; and Professor Emerita, Archaeology and Classical Studies, Wilfrid Laurier University (Waterloo, ON N2L 3C5 Canada)

[2] van der Steen 2004.

[3] Sites in the Jordan Valley that reflect Ammonite ceramic styles and a diversified material culture are not included in this study.

[4] Certain sites currently being excavated are not adequately published for a full appreciation of their figurine assemblages.

[5] A complete and more in-depth study and illustration of the ceramic figurines and statues from WT-13 is currently in preparation by the author with a comprehensive Jordanian corpus forthcoming by R. Hunziker-Rodewald. Preliminary studies by this author include Daviau 1997, 2001, 2006, 2008; Daviau and Dion 1994, 2002; Daviau and Steiner 2000.

[6] Daviau 2001.

[7] Abou Assaf 1980, Dornemann 1983.

[8] For an initial study of zoomorphic figurines from Ammonite sites, see `Amr (1980) and the preliminary reports of excavations at Tall al-`Umayri (for example, Dabrowski 1997)

[9] These same forming techniques are attributed by J. Karageorghis (1999) to figurines of the Cypro-Archaic period on Cyprus.

[10] The flute player from Jalul is shown here with permission from the excavator (after, Younker et al 1996, pl. 12).

[11] Albright 1939, pl. A.

[12] Loud 1948, pl. 242:13, 14.

[13] Shai et al 2011, fig. 11. Even in this small corpus, one figurine has a rounded back with the result that the head is bent forward (ibid., fig. 11.1).

[14] Dabrowski 1997.

[15] For the online catalogue of figurines, see DigMaster@www.cobb.msstate.edu. In his report on the Zaraqun survey, Kamlah illustrates two plaques from northern Jordan (1993, fig. 2) and compares them to various types from Cisjordan (1993,   pp.122–125, fig. 8).

[16] Dabrowski 2009, p. 64 noted incisions around the eyes of a pillar figurine recovered at Hesban (74.3202).

[17] Herr and Clark 2003, figs. 23, 24.

[18] Worschech 1995, p. 187.

[19] Kletter 1996, fig. 6, identifies these mold-made heads as Types B.3.B, b.3.C, B.6.C and B.2.G.

[20] Thareani 2011, figs. 3.76–3.80.

[21] Glueck 1970, fig. 94.

[22] M2001, Saller 1966, fig. 28:2. Heads with pinched faces (Kletter 1996, fig. 4:1, Type A), such as those found at Judean sites (Thareani 2011, figs. 3.81, 3.82), are not represented in Transjordan.

[23] Worschech 1995, figs. 2, 4a, b.

[24] Harding 1950, pl. 15:12.

[25] F33; Koutsoukou and Najjar 1997, fig. 8.

[26] Glueck 1934, fig. 6.

[27] Koutsoukou and Najjar 1997, fig. 8.

[28] Herr and Platt 2002, fig. 16.36:1848.

[29] TJ 1877, Daviau 2002, fig. 2.34:1.

[30] Although its position suggests a rider, the fact that WT 439 appears to be naked and retains no evidence that it was attached to a horse mitigates this interpretation.

[31] TJ 1119, Daviau 2002, fig. 2.31:1.

[32] Daviau 2002, pp. 53–58, fig. 2.28:1.

[33] Sedman 2002.

[34] One 'figurine' (U1696) may in fact be a statue fragment although this cannot be confirmed from the illustration (Herr and Platt 2002, fig. 16.36:1696).

[35] Bienkowski 1995.

[36] For a complete bibliography prior to 1999, see Daviau 2001; examples of more recent studies include Mansour 2005 for `Amman, Dabrowski 2009 for Tall al-`Umayri, Sedman 2002 for Busayra and the synthetic study of Sugimoto 2008.

[37] Ḥorvat Qitmit; Cohen/Yisraeli 1995 and `En Ḥaṣeva; Beck 1995.

[38] Glueck 1970, fig. 90.

[39] I am grateful to Jonathan Ferguson of the Tell Madaba Project who first brought this statue to my attention.

[40] Petit et al 2006,187; fig. 4.

[41] Glueck 1951, fig. 13.

[42] Gunneweg and Balla 2002; Gunneweg and Mommsen 1990, 1995.

[43] Gunneweg and Balla, personal communication.

[44] Sugimoto 2008.

[45] Younker et al 1996, pl. 12.

[46] Koutsoukou and Najjar 1997, fig. 2.

[47] Frevel 2008.

[48] Guy 1939, pl. 24: M 4385.

[49] Karageorghis 1999, pls. I–XV.

[50] If not the goddess herself, these figures may be lesser goddesses associated with the cult of the higher deity. For a different opinion, see Sugimoto 2008, p. 85, who understands the disc-holding females, even those that appear naked, as "human women" who represented the goddess (Astarte).

[51] Kletter 1996.

[52] Stager 1982, p.119, n. 34; Ackerman 2003, pp. 463–465; Hestrin 1987; Kletter 1996.

[53] Daviau 2002, fig. 2.29:1.

[54] Dornemann 1983, 88:3.

[55] Beck 1993.

[56] Pesce 1965.

[57] Daviau 2001.

BIBLIOGRAPHY

Abou Assaf 1980	Abou Assaf, A. *Untersuchungen zur Ammonitischen Rundbildkunst. Ugarit-Forschungen* 12, pp. 7–102.
Ackerman 2003	Ackerman, S., "At Home with the Goddess," in *Symbiosis, Symbolism, and the Power of the Past: Canaan, Ancient Israel, and Their Neighbors from the Late Bronze Age through Roman Palaestina*. Proceedings of the Centennial Symposium, W. F. Albright Institute of Archaeological Research and American Schools of Oriental Research, Jerusalem, May 29–31, 2000, W. G. Dever, S. Gitin (eds.), Winona Lake, IN: Eisenbrauns, pp. 455–468.
Albright 1939	Albright, W. F., "Astarte Plaques and Figurines from Tell Beit Mirsim," in *Mélanges Syriens offerts à Monsieur René Dussaud*. Tome Premier. Paris: Librairie Orientaliste Paul Geuthner, pp. 107–120.
`Amr 1980	`Amr, A.-J., *A Study of the Clay Figurines and Zoomorphic Vessels of Trans-Jordan during the Iron Age, with Special Reference to their Symbolism and Function*. Unpublished Ph.D. dissertation, University of London.
Beck 1993	Beck, P., "Transjordanian and Levantine Elements in the Iconography of Qitmit," in *Biblical Archaeology Today 1990*, Proceedings of the Second International Congress on Biblical Archaeology. June–July 1990: Jerusalem: Israel Exploration Society, pp. 231–236.
Beck 1995	Beck, P., "Catalogue of Cult Objects and Study of the Iconography," in *Ḥorvat Qitmit*, pp. 27–197.
Bienkowski 1995	Bienkowski, P., "The Small Finds," in C.-M. Bennett and P. Bienkowski, *Excavations at Tawilan in Southern Jordan*, British Academy Monographs in Archaeology, No. 8. Oxford: Oxford University Press, pp. 79–92.

Busayra	*Busayra, Excavation by Cristal-M. Bennett 1971–1980*, P. Bienkowski (ed.), British Academy Monographs in Archaeology No. 13, Oxford University Press.
Cohen and Yisraeli 1995	Cohen, R., Yisraeli, Y., "The Iron Age Fortresses at `En Ḥaṣeva," *Biblical Archaeologist* 58, pp. 223–235.
Dabrowski 1997	Dabrowski, B.,"Clay Figurines from Tall al-`Umayri and Vicinity (The 1987 and 1989 Seasons)," in *Madaba Plains Project 3. The 1989 Season at Tell el-`Umeiri and Vicinity and Subsequent Studies*, L. G. Herr et al (eds.), Berrien Springs, MI: Andrews University Press, pp. 337–349.
Dabrowski 2009	Dabrowski, B.,"Terracotta Figurines From Tell Hesban and Vicinity," in *Small Finds: Studies of Bone, Iron, Glass, Figurines, and Stone Objects from Tell Hesban and Vicinity. Hesban 12.* Berrien Springs, MI: Andrews University Press, pp. 59–89.
Daviau 1997	Daviau, P. M. M., "Moab's Northern Border: Khirbat al-Mudayna on the Wadi ath-Thamad," *Biblical Archaeologist* 60, pp. 222–228.
Daviau 2002	Daviau, P. M. M., *Excavations at Tall Jawa, Jordan* II, *The Iron Age Artefacts*, Culture and History of the Ancient Near East 11/2. Leiden: Brill.
Daviau 2006	Daviau, P. M. M.,"Ḥirbet el-Mudēyine in its Landscape: Iron Age Towns, Forts, and Shrines," *Zeitschrift des Deutschen Palästina-Veriens* 122, pp. 14–30.
Daviau 2008	Daviau, P. M. M., "Ceramic Architectural Models from Transjordan and the Syrian Tradition," in *Proceedings of the 4th International Congress,* pp. 293–30.
Daviau and Dion 1994	Daviau, P. M. M., Dion, P.-E., "El, the God of the Ammonites? The *Atef*-Crowned Head from Tell Jawa, Jordan," *Zeitschrift des Deutschen Palästina-Vereins* 110, pp.1–3.
Daviau and Dion, 2002	Daviau, P. M. M., Dion, P.-E., "Moab Comes to Light," *Biblical Archaeology Review* 28/1, pp. 38–49, 63.
Daviau and Steiner 2000	Daviau, P. M. M., Steiner, M. L., "A Moabite Sanctuary at Khirbat al–Mudayna," *Bulletin of the American Schools of Oriental Research* 320, pp. 1–21.
Dornemann 1983	Dornemann, R., *The Archaeology of the Transjordan in the Bronze and Iron Ages*, Milwaukee: Milwaukee Public Museum.
Frevel 2008	Frevel, C., "Gifts to the Gods? Votives as Communication Markers in Sanctuaries and other Places in the Bronze and Iron Ages in Palestine/Israel," in *From Ebla to Stellenbosch, Syro-Palestinian Religions and the Hebrew Bible*, I. Cornelius, L. Jonker (eds.), Wiesbaden: Harrassowitz Verlag, pp. 25–48.
Glueck 1934	Glueck, N., *Explorations in Eastern Palestine* I, *Annual of the American Schools of Oriental Research* 14 (1933–1944), Philadelphia: American Schools of Oriental Research.
Glueck 1951	Glueck, N., *Explorations in Eastern Palestine* IV, Annual of the American Schools of Oriental Research 25–28 (1945–49). Philadelphia: American Schools of Oriental Research.
Glueck 1970	Glueck, N., *The Other Side of the Jordan*, Cambridge, MA: American Schools of Oriental Research.
Gunneweg and Balla 2002	Gunneweg, J., Balla, M., "Instrumental Neutron Activation Analysis, Busayra and Judah," in, *Busayra,* pp. 483–486.
Gunneweg and Mommsen 1990	Gunneweg, J., Mommsen, H., "Instrumental Neutron Activation Analysis and the origin of some cult objects and Edomite vessels from the Horvat Qitmit Shrine," *Archaeometry* 32, pp. 7–18.
Gunneweg and Mommsen 1995	Gunneweg, J. and H. Mommsen, "Instrumental Neutron Activation Analysis of vessels and Cult Objects," in *Ḥorvat Qitmit,* pp. 280–287.
Guy 1935	Guy, H. G., *Material Remains of the Megiddo Cult.* OPI 26. Chicago: University of Chicago.
Harding 1950	Harding, G. L., "An Iron-Age Tomb at Meqabelein," *Quarterly of the Department of Antiquities of Palestine* 14, pp. 44–48.
Herr and Clark 2003	Herr, L., Clark, D., "Mādabā Plains Project: Excavations at Tall al-`Umayrī, 2002," *Annual of the Department of Antiquities of Jordan* 47, pp. 279–294.

Herr and Platt 2002	Herr, L. G., Platt, E. E., "The Objects from the 1989 Season," in *The 1994 Season at Tall al-`Umayri and Subsequent Studies. Madaba Plains Project* 5, L. G. Herret et al (eds.), Berrien Springs: Andrews University Press, pp. 358–399.
Hestrin 1987	Hestrin, R., "The Lachish Ewer and the `Asherah," *Israel Exploration Journal* 37, pp. 212–223.
Ḥorvat Qitmit	*Ḥorvat Qitmit. An Edomite Shrine in the Biblical Negev*, I. Beit-Arieh (ed.), Monograph Series of the Institute of Archaeology, 11. Tel Aviv: Tel Aviv University.
Kamlah 1993	Kamlah, J., "Tell el-Fuḫḫār (Zarqu?) und dei pflanzenhaltende Göttin in Palästina. Ergebnisse de Zeraqōn-Surveys 1989," *Zeitschrift des Deutschen Palästina-Veriens* 109, pp. 101–127.
Karageorghis 1999	Karageorghis, J., *The Coroplastic Art of Ancient Cyprus*, V. *The Cypro-Archaic Period, Small Female Figurines*: B. *Figurines moulées*. Nicosia: A. G. Leventis Foundation.
Koutsoukou and Najjar 1997	Koutsoukou, A., Najjar, M., "Figurines," in *The Great Temple of Amman. The Excavations*, A. Koutsoukou et al (eds.), Amman: American Center of Oriental Research, pp. 127–134.
Loud 1948	Loud, G., *Megiddo* II. *Seasons of 1935–1939*, Oriental Institute Publications, Vol. 62. Chicago: University of Chicago Press.
Mansour 2005	Mansour, S., "Figurines and Iron Age Objects from `Ammān Citadel," *Annual of the Department of Antiquities of Jordan* 49, pp. 541–555.
Pesce 1965	Pesce, G., *Le statuette puniche di Bithia*, Serie Archeologica 7, Roma: Centro di Studi Semitici.
Petit et al 2006	Petit, L. et al, "Dayr `Allā Regional Project: Settling the Steppe Second Campaign 2005," *Annual of the Department of Antiquities of Jordan* 50, pp. 179–188.
Saller 1966	Saller, S., "The Iron Age Tombs at Nebo, Jordan, *Liber Annuus* 16, pp. 165–298.
Sedman 2002	Sedman, L., "The Small Finds," in P. Bienkowski, *Busayra*, pp. 353–428.
Shai et al 2011	Shai, I. et al, "Differentiating between Public and Residential Buildings: A Case Study from Late Bronze Age II Tell eṣ-Ṣafi/Gath," in *Household Archaeology in Ancient Israel and Beyond*, A. Yasur-Landau et al (eds.) CHANE 50. Leiden/Boston: Brill, pp. 107–131.
Stager 1982	Stager, L. E., "The Archaeology of the East Slope of Jerusalem and the Terraces of the Kedron," *Journal of Near Eastern Studies* 41, pp. 111–121.
Sugimoto 2008	Sugimoto, D. T., "Female Figurines with a Disk from the Southern Levant and the Formation of Monotheism," Tokyo: Keio University Press.
Thareani 2011	Thareani, Y., *Tel `Aroer. The Iron Age II Caravan Town and the Hellenistic-Early Roman Settlement The Avraham Biran (1975–1982) and Rudolph Cohen (1975–1976) Excavations*, 2 vols. Annual of the Nelson Glueck School of Biblical Archaeology, No. VIII. Jerusalem: Hebrew Union College-Jewish Institute of Religion.
van der Steen 2004	van der Steen, E., *Tribes and Territories in Transition. The central east Jordan Valley and surrounding regions in the Late Bronze and Early Iron Ages: a study of the sources*, Orientalia Lovaniensia Analecta 130; Leuven: Peeters Publishers.
Worschech 1995	Worschech, U., "Figurinen aus el-Balu` (Jordanien)," *Zeitschrift des Deutschen Palästina-Vereins* 111, pp. 185–192.
Younker et al 1996	Younker, R. W. et al, "Preliminary Report of the 1994 Season of the Madaba Plains Project: Regional Survey, Tall al-`Umayri, and Tall Jalul Excavations (June 15–August 30, 1994)," *Andrews University Seminary Studies* 34, pp. 65–92.

P. M. Michele Daviau, Professor Emerita
Wilfrid Laurier University
micheledaviaudion@yahoo.ca

SEEING DOUBLE
VIEWING AND RE-VIEWING JUDEAN PILLAR FIGURINES THROUGH MODERN EYES
Erin D. Darby

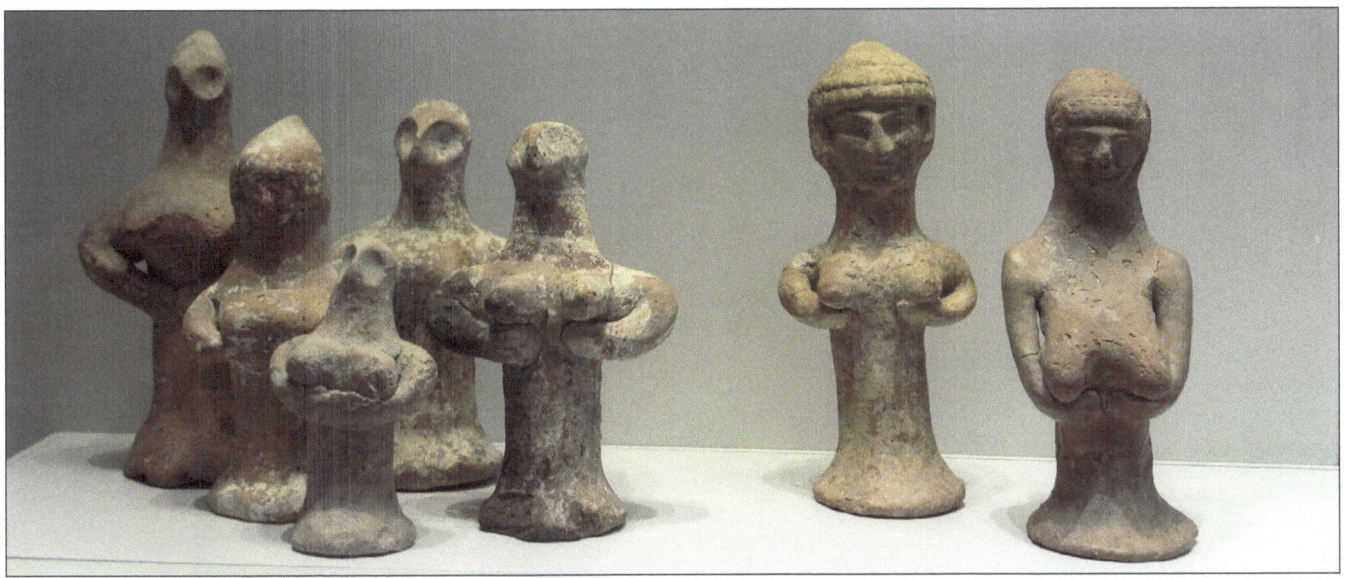

Fig. 1. Pinched head and molded head Judean pillar figurines from the Israel Museum. Photo: Wikimedia Commons

ABSTRACT

Although figurines are usually treated as coherent symbols rather than compilations of separate elements, when it comes to Judean pillar figurines from southern Israel, this approach has failed to generate a scholarly consensus about the figurines' identity and function. Rather than focus on the identity of the figurine, it is time to explore a different methodology by investigating the various individual parts that constitute figurine iconography, including iconographic content, stylistic criteria, and technological characteristics. Because these figurines represent a new combination of elements taken from a variety of earlier artistic tropes and media, this approach takes seriously the process whereby artisan tradition selected separate elements and recombined them into a new whole. In order to demonstrate this methodology, the following paper investigates the pillar bases of the figurines from Jerusalem, evaluating each element according to two design principles—permanence and detail. As a result, these criteria reveal an internal hierarchy that governs the way elements work together to create figurine form and function. Only after this relative hierarchy is observed is it possible to understand whether a figurine was merely a hyper-redundant combination of individual symbols, or whether its elements coalesced to form a unique, holistic image.

INTRODUCTION

Although visual experience is often overlooked as a straight-forward process, the acts of seeing and interpreting are some of the most complicated functions performed by the human mind.[1] In actuality, images are constituted by a myriad of separate elements, and the means by which an audience perceives these individual elements as a whole is thus negotiable, dependent upon time, space, and culture.[2] Therefore, a modern audience and an ancient audience would not necessarily share the same view.

As one type of image, figurines are composed of many individual properties, both aesthetic and physical. In particular, Judean pillar figurines from the Iron IIB-C in southern Israel are composed of pillar bodies, arms and breasts, and two different styles of heads, as well as clay, whitewash, and paint (see Figs. 1–4). The relative hierarchy of these elements and their meaning for figurine function should not be taken for granted.

Nevertheless, modern interpreters of the Judean corpus often think of various figurine elements as a coherent whole rather than a combination of individual parts. This, in turn, leads interpreters to connect the figurines with goddess worship, as they attempt to

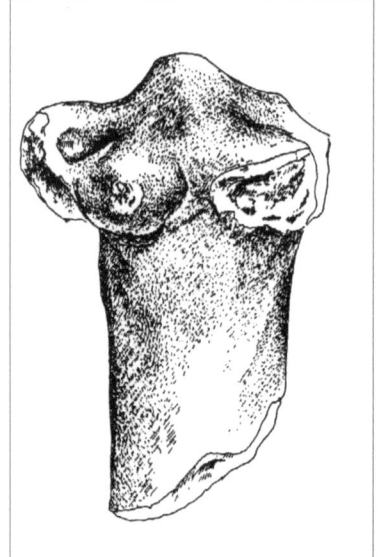

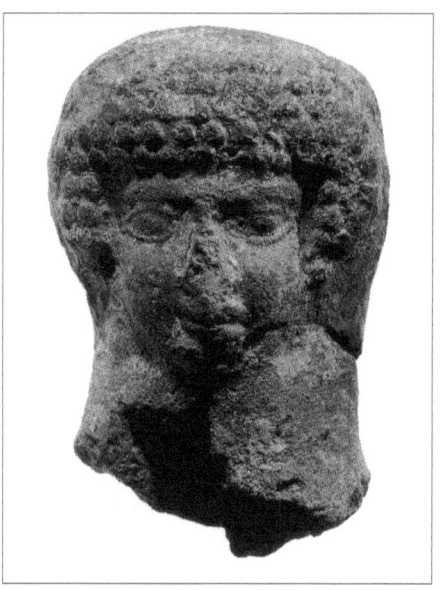

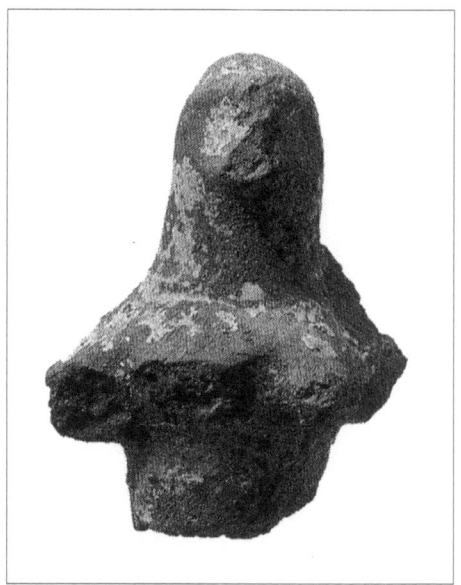

Fig. 2. Drawing of a pillar body with arms supporting the breasts, courtesy of the Institute of Archaeology, Hebrew University of Jerusalem.

Fig. 3. A molded head, courtesy of the Institute of Archaeology, Hebrew University of Jerusalem.

Fig. 4. A pinched head, courtesy of the Institute of Archaeology, Hebrew University of Jerusalem.

identify the one figure that the image is meant to represent. Yet, throughout this interpretive process, certain elements of figurine iconography become the focus of analysis, such as the pillar bases. Often seen as one of the clues that unlock the figurines' identity, pillar bases are used as load-bearing supports to prop up scholarly reconstructions, despite the fact that the relative importance of the bases within the overall figurine iconography is far from certain. Moreover, because Judean pillar figurines are the most common "religious" artifacts from southern Israel in this period, these interpretations strongly influence both scholarly and popular reconstructions of Israelite religion in the Iron Age.[3]

In order to evaluate the manner in which Judean pillar figurines are perceived and interpreted, this paper assesses several figurine elements based on two design principles—permanence and detail. Focusing on the way stylistic and technological features are combined to form the pillar base of the figurines from Jerusalem, the paper suggests that modern interpretations of such elements are often wanting. In contrast, when the figurine bases are considered in light of iconographic form, technological style, and related coroplastic objects, it becomes clear that the base of the figurine may be unrelated to the "identity" of the object, or it may indicate a protective function.

METHODOLOGY

A Judean pillar figurine is constituted by many separate parts that create its subject matter and style. Unfortunately, the process by which these separate parts are combined is largely overlooked. For example, in the field of biblical studies, the iconographic school has been responsible for the resurging interest in ancient Near Eastern art and the Bible; but these interpreters focus on the "meaning" behind visual symbols rather than the manner of their creation.[4]

While the investigation of iconographic content is certainly significant, elements may be included in a representation for a number of reasons; and the most stereotyped aspects of an image are often the most difficult to translate. Focusing on common iconographic elements of figurine design, to the exclusion of other figurine components, such as style, inadvertently creates the impression of a continuous function and meaning that glosses over the particularities of a trope's adaptation in various cultures and time periods.[5]

An alternative to this approach is to include elements of style in the discussion—the particular ways figurine elements were created and incorporated.[6] This would include the often overlooked category of "technological style," which considers the production of images and the effect of production steps on the final product.[7]

Although various aspects of technological style could be explained via a functionalist approach, i.e., economic necessity or resource availability, certain materials and production processes were chosen for ideological reasons as well.[8]

The ideological motivations for production strategies are further supported by the scale and nature of the figurines as miniatures.[9] A miniature is not the same as a replica. While a replica, or a model, attempts to reproduce even the smallest details of a larger image, a miniature is selective, often reproducing only those elements that communicate the most important aspects of the image. Miniatures imply choice on the part of the artisan community, including which visual representations to use, the degree of detail, or energy, invested in any given aspect of the image, and the resources dedicated to the durability of these various parts. Furthermore, miniatures depicting the human body are especially indicative of artistic choice, including which elements are depicted, how they are portrayed, and which elements remain ambiguous.[10]

THE TECHNOLOGICAL STYLE OF JUDEAN PILLAR FIGURINES

Judean pillar figurines are composed of fired clay, white wash, and paint. Rated on a continuum of permanence or durability, clay is certainly less durable than stone or metal, and this suggests the figurines were not created for extensive, long-term use. At the same time, artisans did dedicate the time and resources to fire the images, indicating that they were intended for some durability. Firing the figurines also implies they may have been manipulated by hand, displayed, and exposed to the air, since unfired clay would disintegrate quickly when handled.[11] Furthermore, those elements made of clay may also have been intended to endure for some time and must have been important to the function and meaning of the image.[12] This would include the heads, particularly the molded faces, the hand-modeled arms and breasts, and the hand-modeled pillar bodies.

The significance of clay as a production material is also indicated by a number of ancient Near Eastern textual witnesses. In addition to clay or earth in creation accounts,[13] clay was an important material in rituals of protection and transference. For example, a number of Mesopotamian ritual texts mention clay and its protective and healing functions. Tablet 9 of the Utukkū Lemnūtu incantations prays, "may Nunurra, the great potter of Anu, drive (the demon) away from the house in a pot fired in a pure kiln from a pure place."[14] From the same corpus, Tablet 12 describes "liquid extract of dark clay" used to cover the outside gate of the temple to protect against demonic attack.[15] Further, raw clay is used in one sky omen NAM.BUR.BI, a ritual used to ward off evil predicted by omens.[16] Additionally, a ritual to ensure healthy delivery requires the woman to recite prayers inside a potter's kiln.[17]

From the Ugaritic corpus, the *Kirtu Epic* describes the god El forming a divine female from clay and commanding her to heal King Kirtu.[18] There also seems to be a connection between potters and healing rituals in Egyptian magico-medical literature,[19] and it has been suggested that this connection should be applied to Egyptian clay female figurines as well.[20] So, too, the Hebrew Bible indicates that clay had unique properties that might be used in rituals transmitting purity and impurity.[21] Nor is this association between clay and ritual properties entirely unique to the ancient Near East.[22] In sum, these various witnesses undergird the conclusions made on stylistic grounds, especially the hypothesis that figurine elements formed in clay would have been important for the figurines' ritual function.

The clay properties can be compared with whitewash and painted decoration. While there is overwhelming evidence that the figurines contained whitewash and paint, these particular elements are poorly preserved on almost all extant exemplars. Whitewash may have served two purposes. It hides imperfections resulting from poorly levigated clay or firing mishaps. Indeed, even badly malformed fragments were covered and used. The whitewash also prepares the surface for painted decoration. Furthermore, other cultic items, such as zoomorphic figurines, cult stands, and shrine boxes, were regularly whitewashed and painted, suggesting some common techniques for the preparation of cultic objects.[23]

Perhaps the best explanation is that whitewash was an appropriate solution for the aesthetic irregularities that accompany clay formation and also provided an appropriate surface for painting.[24] Because clay was necessary for the figurines' function, whitewash was the easiest way to improve their appearance. That having been said, ethnographic analogy suggests that whitewash and paint quickly fade from

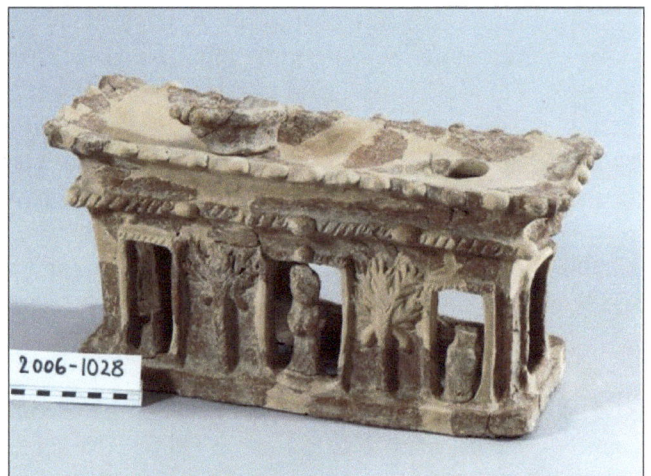

(Left) Fig. 5. Example of a Yavneh cult stand with pillar-based female. Courtesy of Raz Kletter. Photo: Leonid Padrul

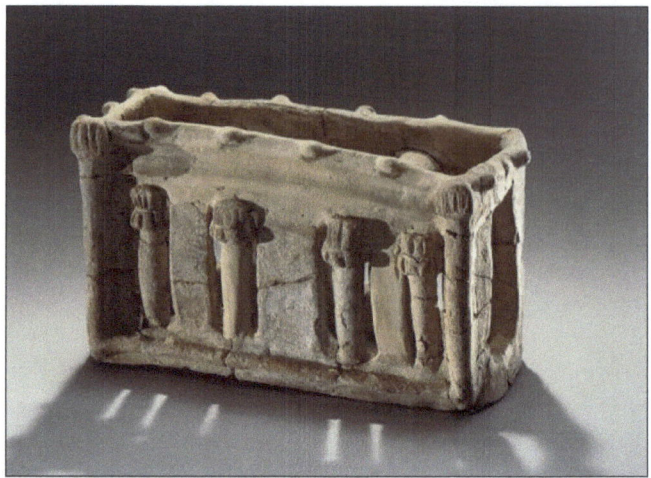

(Right) Fig. 6. Example of a Yavneh cult stand with pillars. Courtesy of Raz Kletter. Photo: Leonid Padrul.

figurines, particularly when exposed to the elements.[25] Thus, while the whitewash and paint must have been important in the initial design and function, they were not the most durable components of the image, which may suggest design elements depicted in paint were only necessary in the initial phase of a figurine ritual. At the same time, those figurine elements that were formed from clay as well as painted, suggesting both durability and detail, would probably be the most important elements within the hierarchy of the image.

PILLAR BASES IN SCHOLARLY OPINION AND STYLISTIC ANALYSIS

Turning to the pillar figurines, most examples from Jerusalem include hand-made, solid pillar bases, though some wheel-made[26] or hollow[27] fragments have also been found. The pillar bases have presented certain complications for the study of pillar figurines. Some interpreters have assumed that the pillar represents a tree trunk, which they connect with Asherah and sacred tree imagery.[28] This opinion remains fairly popular, despite the fact that the definition of the biblical terminology purportedly related to the goddess is still debated,[29] and the connection between the goddess Asherah and trees has been complicated.[30]

Other interpreters have argued that the plain bases should be contrasted with the figurines' Canaanite forerunners—the naked female plaque figurines. Such scholars claim that the pillar base is evidence for a distinction between Canaanite "fertility" figurines and Judean "nurturing" figurines, which emphasize a nursing mother rather than a "courtesan of the gods."[31] In

this view, either the figurines are wearing a dress, or the schematic nature of the lower body was meant to censor elements from Canaanite religion, such as the pudenda.

The first and most practical objection to either of these approaches is that pillar bases are common on a number of figurines all over the world as a means to support a standing image,[32] suggesting that a more functional rationale cannot be dismissed. Further, pillar bases are component parts of a number of figurines both in the Middle Bronze Age in the ancient Near East, as well as in contemporaneous figurine traditions from Philistia,[33] Ammon,[34] Moab,[35] Northern Israel,[36] Cyprus,[37] and Phoenicia.[38] Thus, there is considerable precedent for adopting a simple and schematic pillar base from the iconographic traditions of the Levant and Cyprus, which does not suggest a unique connection between Judean pillar figurines and sacred tree iconography assumed to be central to Asherah worship as depicted in the Bible.

Going beyond these practical considerations, stylistic features present problems for these common interpretations. First, the pillar bases generally lack molded decoration or any modeling that indicates the pillar was intended to represent either a tree or a garment. Second, in many examples only whitewash remains; where paint is preserved it consists of broad stripes in red and yellow.[39] In short, the paint may simply depict geometric designs, as is the case on some Philistine hand-made figurines.[40] This lack of paint on the pillars should be contrasted with the faces and chests of Judean pillar figurines, where the remains of red, black, and yellow paint have been found with some regularity.[41] Finally, were the pillar meant to represent a clothed female body, this artistic convention would differ considerably from that in neighboring Egypt, where clothing on females is most frequently depicted adhering closely to the body, so much so that the breasts, waist, thighs, buttocks, and even pubic triangle remain visible.[42] Given the fact that Egyptian convention largely governs the art of the Levant from this period, the schematic nature of the pillar base is even more striking.

Nor does the technological style of the pillars suggest that the pillar was one of the most essential aspects of the figurines. As part of the overall design, pillars are made of poorly-levigated clay, with consistent grey-coring that indicates they may not have been properly fired or were used as filler in kilns. Even when the pillar base is bent or disfigured the figurine is not discarded, but is whitewashed and used regardless.[43] Clearly the condition of the pillar was not so significant as to interfere with the object's function.

In sum, the fact that pillars were formed and fired as a part of the entire figurine suggests that they may have functioned either as a stand for the image or that the image could be held in the hand without breaking or disintegrating immediately. In other words, they do reflect a certain permanence or durability. However, when the technological characteristics are considered in combination with the lack of detail in molding, modeling, or painting, the pillars are certainly less important than other aspects of the image. As such, the pillar base is an unlikely place to look for the key that identifies the figurines' identity.

COMPARANDA

Comparing the pillar bases to related coroplastic objects also helps to clarify their relative importance and function. In addition to the pillar-based figurines outside of Judah, a number of pillar-style figurines, including those with hands on their breasts, were attached to the cult stands in the Yavneh corpus, found along the Mediterranean coast of Philistia.[45] These stands were dated to the end of the 9th through the beginning of the 8th centuries B.C.[46] and thus bridge the gap between the plaque figurines of the Late Bronze Age and the pillar figurines of the Iron IIB-C (Fig. 5).

As to the pillar-based females on the Yavneh cult stands, Irit Ziffer has explained the pillar base as a skirt, suggesting a partially dressed female.[47] This is problematic for several reasons. While it is true that females holding their breasts are more frequently depicted with fully-formed lower bodies on these cult stands,[48] these frontally molded or modeled females appear in the same areas of the cult stands (in rectangular or rounded openings) and with the same gestures as the females with pillar bases, suggesting a similar function.

Furthermore, females are not the only figures attached to the Yavneh cult stands by means of a pillar or peg. Zoomorphic fragments are also depicted by their heads or heads and pegs, attached vertically in the openings.[49] Moreover, in many of the same openings, the space is filled by pillar columns.[50] Thus, it makes the most sense to read the pillar bases on the females in the same way one reads the pillar bases on zoomorphic images and columns—namely, as architectural features (Fig. 6).

Nor is the Yavneh corpus alone in combining female figurines with architectural features. Other cult stands also use frontally molded females or sphinxes with molded heads as a substitute for columns; the heads may be associated with capitols and volutes.[51] In fact, frontally-molded, naked females commonly flank doorways and stand-in for architectural elements on cult shrines and stands from the Middle Bronze through the Iron Age, a fact already noted by Silvia Schroer.[52]

Although Schroer is aware of the potential connection between Judean pillar bases and columns, she interprets the base of the figurine as the trunk of a tree, assuming the figurines are associated with the goddess Asherah, who she connects with tree iconography. At the same time, however, she argues that frontally-molded, naked female bodies on cult stands and shrine boxes often represent architectural elements; and, in these cases, she argues that the females served as guardian figurines, similar to the protective *lamassu* and *šēdu*.[53] Given the fact that frontally-molded and pillar-based females seem to have been used interchangeably on the Yavneh cult stands, it makes more sense to argue that both the pillar-based females on the Yavneh stands and the Judean pillar figurines are alternative versions of the same protective female figures.

As to the function of the Yavneh cult items in particular, although Raz Kletter identifies these cult stands as

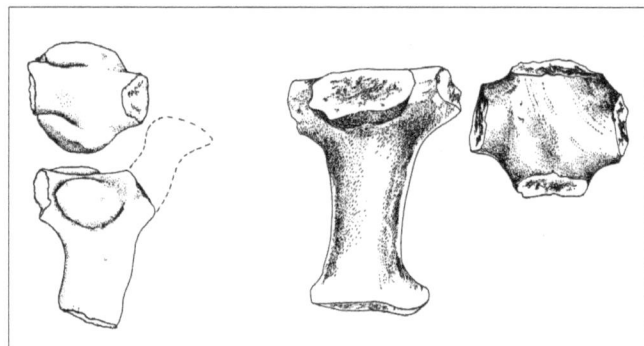

Fig. 7. Detail drawing of bird pillar figurines, courtesy of the Institute of Archaeology, Hebrew University of Jerusalem

votive objects left in a temple (as yet undiscovered) and used for a number of purposes,[54] he also notes that they depict architectural elements used in the construction of sacred spaces.[55] Unfortunately, Kletter then claims the females on the cult stands may represent the consort of the god worshipped in the temple space, depicted because "the god prefers nice, erotic images of his consort, rather than of himself, on his gifts."[56] In contrast, many of the images on the cult stands, such as sphinxes, lions, bulls, caprids, and trees, are known in larger media from elsewhere in the ancient Near East, particularly temple and palace architecture, where they may function as images of protection and blessing.[57] Because the females, with or without pillar bases, were adopted on the cult stands along with other protective characters, the best explanation might be that they serve an apotropaic function, as divine guardian figures. This would be in keeping with Schroer's interpretation of other cultic items in which frontally molded females stand in for architectural features as protective guardians.

Finally, whether the pillar bases are meant to recall actual pillars or merely represent a schematization of a relatively unimportant lower body, ancient Near Eastern artistic style presents some precedent for excerpting symbols from their original settings, such as torsos with hands holding the breasts, and recombining them in new ways, like adding this trope to a pillar base. For example, Egyptian depictions of Hathor frequently borrowed only the head or the head and bust of the image in a type of synecdoche to indicate the meaning of the total image.[58] Similarly, ancestor statues at Deir el-Medina consisted of busts alone; clearly the bottom section of the image was simply unnecessary.[59] Furthermore, this abbreviated form of the female image combined with other elements, like wings or a sun disc, is also known from Syrian and Phoenician art of the Iron II.[60] In Egyptian iconography the extraction of particular symbols of gods and their recombination into fantastical forms may even have increased the effectiveness of an image.[61] Moreover, Andrzej Niwiński argues that the media of miniatures (here specifically scarabs and coffins of the 21st Dynasty) requires that images be abbreviated, what he calls the *pars pro toto* rule.[62]

This method also occurs in large-scale art. Female images combined with actual columns are known from Hathor columns in Egypt[63] and at Timnah,[64] as well as the basalt female standing on the back of a lion from the ninth century palace entrance at Tell Halaf.[65] Caryatids, believed to have been influenced by Ionic temples in Anatolia, may be a later continuation of these Syrian and Anatolian traditions.[66]

Thus, most of the comparanda agree with the conclusions based on stylistic criteria and suggest that the lower "body" of the figurine is actually a pillar and a schematization that has largely lost its significance for the function of this image. In comparison, a number of free-standing bird figurines appended to pillars have been discovered throughout Judah,[67] although few scholars would argue that the pillar is anything more than the base of the figurine (Fig. 7). These bird figurines come from the same region, time period, and sites as Judean pillar figurines. If the bases of Judean figurines maintain any significance, perhaps they recall the pillar columns from protective figures on cult stands guarding shrine spaces. Such an interpretation would be consistent with descriptions of clay in ancient Near Eastern texts that indicate its association with protection and healing.

SUMMARY AND CONCLUSIONS

This examination of the pillar bases on Judean-style pillar figurines has revealed that the technological characteristics, stylistic criteria, and related coroplastic objects all yield a similar interpretation—namely that the bases of the figurines were not only the least important iconographic elements in the figurine design but that their schematization and ambivalence actually indicate some connection with shrine box and cult stand iconography where female guardian figures typically take the place of architectural elements. In contrast, by attempting to read all figurine elements together as representing a single character, scholars consistently misread the iconography. The resulting interpretations either insist the pillar bases, as part of a coherent symbol, represent tree trunks whose meaning is unlocked by an assumed relationship between the biblical terminology describing Asherah and a possible connection between the goddess and trees, or insist that the pillar base was incorporated into the holistic image as a garment meant to contrast the Judean figurines with their lascivious counterpart in Canaanite mythology.

The problem with Judean pillar figurines has always been the absence of a direct iconographic antecedent in any material or medium. The advent of these clay figurines appears to represent a new creation taken from individually known elements. Thus, whether this creation intends to suggest one holistic image, for example, that of a recognizable super-natural being, is not readily apparent. The alternative, tracking the individual design components, their stylistic characteristics, and their unique combination, still suggests a tentative but informed function for the image, as one intended to protect and preserve. It may also suggest that the extended search for the figurines' "identity" is misguided.

NOTES

[1] Kuehni 2012, pp. 424–428; Yu 2012, pp. 292–299; Barat 2007, pp. 228–251; Donderi 2006, pp. 73–97; Greisdorf and O'Conner 2002, pp. 6–29; Albright and Stoner 2002, pp. 333–379.

[2] Mamassian 2008, pp. 2143–2153.

[3] Kletter 1996, pp. 10–27; Darby 2011, pp. 69–108.

[4] Weissenrieder 2009, p. 117; LeMon 2010, pp. 146–147; Winter 2010a, p. 139.

[5] Bal 1991; Keel 1992a, pp. 267–271; Keel 1992b, pp. 360–361; Keel 1998; Keel and Uehlinger 1998, pp. 12–13; De Hulster 2009, p. 146; Winter 2010a, pp. 140–141.

[6] Conkey 1989, pp, 118–129; Wobst 1999, pp. 118–132; Winter 2010b, p. 34; Winter 2010c, pp. 407, 421–422.

[7] Reedy and Reedy 1994, pp. 304–320; Stark 1998, pp. 1–11; Petty 2006, p. 21.

[8] Hardin 1996, p. 47; Stark 1998, pp. 1–11; Hegmon 1998, pp. 264–280; Gosselain 2000, pp. 187–217.

[9] Bailey 2005, pp. 32–33; Smith 2009, pp. 18–21; Winter 2010a, pp. 142–143, 147.

[10] Joyce 1993, pp. 255–274; Kuijt and Chesson 2005, pp. 152–183.

[11] Van Buren 1930, pp. 191–192, 211.

[12] Petty 2006, p. 25; Bailey 2005, p. 98.

[13] Barrelet 1968, pp. 7–11; Ritner 1993, pp. 137–138; Dorman 2002, pp. 113–132; Darby 2011, pp. 411–412.

[14] Geller 2007, p. 228, Tablet 9:47.

[15] Geller 2007, pp. 240–241, Tablet 12:92–94.

[16] Maul 1994, p. 457.

[17] Scurlock 2002, p. 219.

[18] Lewis 2005, p. 98; Darby 2011, pp. 508–509.

[19] Dorman 2002, pp. 30, 96.

[20] Waraksa 2009.

[21] Darby 2011, pp. 435–442.

[22] Hardin 1996, p. 40; Huyler 1994, p. 325.

[23] E.g., Kletter and Ziffer 2010, CAT 80, pl. 116; CAT 82, pl. 5:3; CAT 95, pls. 129–130; CAT112, pl. 143:1.

[24] Cf. Deut 27:1–6 and Tigay 1996, p. 248.

[25] Weinberg 1965, p. 191; Blurton 1997, p. 175; Ziffer 2010, p. 9.

[26] Kletter 1996, Appendix 5, 5.I.2.2–4, 8; Kletter 1996, Addenda to Appendix 2: 764.C.3.

[27] Kletter 1996, Appendix 5: 5.I.2.7; Kletter 1996, Appendix 2: 306.C.1.

[28] E.g., Kelso and Thorley 1943, p. 138; Hestrin 1991, p. 57; Bloch-Smith 1992, p. 99; Uehlinger 1997, pp. 100, 142; Keel 1998, pp. 20–46.

[29] E.g., Olyan 1988, pp. 70–74; Day 2000, pp. 42–48, 51; Hadley 2000, pp. 54–83; Zevit 2000, pp. 650–651; Smith 2002, pp. 119–133; Mastin 2004, pp. 326–351; Dever 2005, pp. 196–208, 211–218; Wiggins 2007, pp. 105–150.

[30] Wiggins 2007, pp. 252, 268–69.

31 Engle 1979, p. 114; Dever 2005, p. 187.

32 Kletter 1996, pp. 76–77.

33 Press 2012, pp. 199, 205–206.

34 'Amr 1980, pp. 22–35.

35 Daviau 2001, p. 322.

36 Kletter 1996, pp. 32–34.

37 Karageorghis 1991, p. 13.

38 Press 2012, p. 172.

39 E.g., Gilbert-Peretz 1996, Reg. G/2281/1.

40 Press 2012, p. 195.

41 E.g., Gilbert-Peretz 1996, Reg. G/4931, E3/12886, E3/13016, E1/6143.

42 Robins 1993, p. 183; Robins 2008, pp. 76, 150, 208.

43 E.g., Gilbert-Peretz 1996, Reg. E1/20526, D2/20573, E2/3893.

44 Darby 2011, pp. 484–486.

45 Kletter and Ziffer 2010, CAT 37, pls. 11:1, 76–77, 78:1–2; CAT 44, pls. 13:1, 84–85; CAT 49, pls. 2:2, bottom, 14:2, 90:1, 3, 91:1; CAT 59 pls. 33:1, 103:2–3.

46 Panitz-Cohen 2010, p. 131.

47 Ziffer 2010, p. 77.

48 Kletter and Ziffer 2010, CAT 84, pls. 21:1, 43:1, bottom, 119, 120:1; CAT 85, pls. 41:1, 120:2–3; CAT 86, pls. 21:2, 121; CAT 92, pls. 23:2, 125:2–3, 126:1–2; CAT 113, pls. 26:1, 143:2, 144; CAT 123, pl. 150:2; CAT 28, pls. 9:2, 69, 70:1; CAT 29, pls. 47:3, 70:2–3; CAT 57, pls. 7:1, 17:2, 99–100; CAT 90, pls. 1:2–3, 40:1–2, 41, 123:3–4.

49 Kletter and Ziffer 2010, CAT 22, pl. 65; CAT 30, pl. 71; CAT 41, pl. 81; CAT 110, pl. 141:2.

50 Kletter and Ziffer 2010, CAT 17, pl. 62:1; CAT 52, pls. 5:1, 16:1, 93:4, 94; CAT 53, pls. 2:2, center, 16:2, 95; CAT 54, pl. 96:1; CAT 106, pl. 138:2.

51 Zevit 2001, pp. 325–326, fig. 4.10; Maeir and Dayagi-Mendels 2007, pp. 111–123, figs. 1, 2.

52 Schroer 2007, pp. 438–439; Rowe 1940, pp. 54–55, pls. 17:1, 57A:1, 35:2, 17:2, 56A: 3; Wooley 1955, pp. 64, 248, pl. 58:a, b; Keel 1998, p. 41; Beck 2002, pp. 185, figs. 1, 2, 3a, 209, fig. 10, 414.

53 Schroer 2007, pp. 430–438.

54 Kletter 2010a, pp. 186–188.

55 Kletter 2010b, pp. 42–43.

56 Kletter 2010a, p. 188.

57 Beck 2002, p. 402; Nevling Porter 2003, pp. 11–37.

58 Robins 2008, p. 175, fig. 206; Staubli 2009, pp. 93–112; abb. 3.

59 Friedman 1994, pp. 111–117; Robins 2008, pp. 189–190.

60 Bisi 1988, figs. 1g, 1d; Gubel 1993, p. 123, figs. 61–63.

61 Hornung 2000, pp. 1–20; Kákosy 2000, pp. 45–49.

62 Niwiński 2000, p. 27.

63 Schroer 2007, pp. 442–443.

64 Rothenberg 1972, pp. 130, 151, fig. 78.

65 Oppenheim 1931, p. 121.

66 Mylonas Shear 1999, pp. 65–85.

67 E.g., Kletter 1996, Appendix 5: 5.II.

BIBLIOGRAPHY

Albright and Stoner 2002 — Albright, T. D., Stoner, G. R., "Contextual Influences on Visual Processing," *Annual Review of Neuroscience* 25, pp. 339–79.

`Amr 1980    `Amr, A-J., *A Study of the Clay Figurines and Zoomorphic Vessels of Trans-Jordan during the Iron Age, with Special Reference to Their Symbolism and Function*, Ph. D. dissertation, University of London.

Bailey 2005   Bailey, D. W., *Prehistoric Figurines: Representation and Corporeality in the Neolithic*, London: Routledge.

Bal 1991   Bal, M., *Reading 'Rembrandt': Beyond the Word-Image Opposition*, Cambridge: Cambridge University Press.

Barat 2007   Barat, A. H., "Human Perception and Knowledge Organization: Visual Imagery," *Library Hi Tech* 25, pp. 338–351.

Beck 2002   Beck, P., *Imagery and Representation: Studies in the Art and Iconography of Ancient Palestine: Collected Articles*, Institute of Archaeology, Tel Aviv University, Occasional Publications 3, Tel Aviv: the Institute of Archaeology, Tel Aviv University.

Bisi 1988   Bisi, A. M., "Antécédents éblaïtes d'un apotropaïon phénico-punique," in *Wirtschaft und Gesellschaft von Ebla: Akten der Internationalen Tagung Heidelberg, 4–7 November 1986*, H. Waetzoldt, H. Hauptmann, (eds.), Heidelberg: Heidelberger Orientverlag, pp. 21–33

Bloch-Smith 1992   Bloch-Smith, E., J*udahite Burial Practices and Beliefs About the Dead*, Journal for the Study of the Old Testament Monograph Series 7; Journal for the Study of the Old Testament Supplement 123, Sheffield: Sheffield Academic Press.

Blurton 1997   Blurton, T. R., "Terracotta Figurines of Eastern Gujarat," in *Pottery in the Making: Ceramic Traditions* I, Freestone, D. Gaimster (eds.), Washington, D. C.: Smithsonian Institution Press, pp. 170–175.

Conkey 1989   Conkey, M. W., "The Use of Diversity in Stylistic Analysis," in *Quantifying Diversity in Archaeology*, R. D. Leonard, G. T. Jones (eds.), Cambridge: Cambridge University Press, pp. 118–129.

Darby 2011   Darby, E., *Interpreting Judean Pillar Figurines: Gender and Empire in Judean Apotropaic Ritual*, Ph. D.dissertation, Duke University.

Day 2000   Day, J., *Yahweh and the Gods and Goddesses of Canaan*, Journal for the Study of the Old Testament Supplement 265, Sheffield: Sheffield Academic Press.

Dever 2005   Dever, W. G., *Did God Have a Wife?: Archaeology and Folk Religion in Ancient Israel*, Grand Rapids, Mich.: Eerdmans.

Donderi 2006   Donderi, D. C., "Visual Complexity: A Review," *Psychological Bulletin* 132, pp. 73–97.

Dorman 2002   Dorman, P. F., "Faces in Clay: Techniques, Imagery, and Allusion in a Corpus of Ceramic Sculpture from Ancient Egypt," in *A Corpus of Ceramic Sculpture from Ancient Egypt*, Münchner Ägyptologische Studien 52, Mainz am Rhein: Philipp von Zabern.

Engle 1979   Engle, J. R., *Pillar Figurines of the Iron Age and Ashera/Asherim*, Ph. D. dissertation, University of Pittsburgh.

Friedman 1994   Friedman, F. D., "Aspects of Domestic Life and Religion," in *Pharaoh's Workers: The Villagers of Deir el Medina*, L. H. Lesko (ed.), Ithaca, N.Y.: Cornell University Press, pp. 95–117.

Geller 2007   Geller, M. J., *Evil Demons: Canonical Utukkū Lemnūtu Incantations: Introduction, Cuneiform Text, and Transliteration with a Translation and Glossary*, State Archives of Assyrian Cuneiform Texts 5, Helsinki: Vammalan Kirjapaino Oy.

Gilbert-Peretz 1996   Gilbert-Peretz, D., "Ceramic Figurines," in *Excavations at the City of David, 1978–1985: Directed by Yigal Shiloh*, Vol. 4: *Various Reports*, D. T. Ariel, A. de Groot (eds.), Qedem 35, Jerusalem: the Hebrew University of Jerusalem, pp. 29–41.

Gosselain 2000   Gosselain, O. P., "Materializing Identities: An African Perspective," J*ournal of Archaeological Method and Theory* 7, pp. 187–217.

Greisdorf and O'Conner 2002   Greisdorf, H., O'Conner, B. C., "Modeling What Users See When They Look at Images: A Cognitive Viewpoint," *Journal of Documentation* 58, pp. 6–29.

Gubel 1993	Gubel, E., "The Iconography of Inscribed Phoenician Glyptic," in *Studies in the Iconography of Northwest Semitic Inscribed Seals: Proceedings of a Symposium Held in Fribourg on April 17–20, 1991*, B. Sass, C. Uehlinger (eds.), Orbis Biblicus et Orientalis 125. Fribourg: University Press, Göttingen: Vandenhoeck & Ruprecht, pp. 101–129.
Hadley 2000	Hadley, J. M., *The Cult of Asherah in Ancient Israel and Judah*, Cambridge: Cambridge University Press.
Hardin 1996	Hardin, K. L., "Technological Style and the Making of Culture: Three Kono Contexts of Production," in *African Material Culture*, M. J. Arnoldi, C. M. Geary, K. L. Hardin (eds.), Bloomington, Ind.: Indiana University Press, pp. 31–50.
Hegmon 1998	Hegmon, M., "Technology, Style, and Social Practices: Archaeological Approaches," in *The Archaeology of Social Boundaries*, M. T. Stark (ed), Washington D.C.: Smithsonian, pp. 264–280.
Hestrin 1991	Hestrin, R., "Understanding Asherah," *Biblical Archaeology Review* 17, pp. 50–59.
Hornung 2000	Hornung, E., "Komposite Gottheiten in der ägyptischen Ikonographie," in *Images as Media*, pp. 1–20.
Hulster 2009	Hulster, I. J. de, "Illuminating Images: A Historical Position and Method for Iconographic Exegesis," in *Iconography and Biblical Studies*, pp. 139–162.
Huyler 1994	Huyler, S. P., "Tulasi: A Survey and Case Study of Ritual Terracotta Planters for Tulasi, the Goddess Incarante as a Basil Bush, in Coastal Orissa, in *Living Traditions, Studies in the Ethnoarchaeology of South Asia*, B. Allchin (ed.), New Delhi, India: Oxford and IBH Publishing, pp. 323–349.
Iconography and Biblical Studies	*Iconography and Biblical Studies: Proceedings of the Iconography Sessions at the Joint EABS/SBL Conference*, (22 July–26 July, 2007), *Vienna, Austria*, I. J. Hulster, R. Schmitt (eds.), Alter Orient und Altes Testament 361, Münster: Ugarit.
Joyce 1993	Joyce, R. A., "Women's Work: Images of Production and Reproduction in Pre-Hispanic Southern Central America," *Current Anthropology* 34, pp. 255–274.
Kákosy 2000	Kákosy, L., "Bermerkungen zur Ikonographie der magischen Heilstatuen," in *Images as Media*, pp. 45–49.
Karageorghis 1991	Karageorghis, V., "The Coroplastic Art of Cyprus: An Introduction," in *Cypriote Terracottas Proceedings of the First International Conference of Cypriote Studies*, Brussels-Liège–Amsterdam, 29 May–1 June 1989, F. Vandenabeele, R. Laffineur, (eds.), Brussels-Liège: A.G. Leventis Foundation, Vrije Universiteit Brussel-Université de Liège, pp. 9–15.
Keel 1992a	Keel, O., *Das Recht der Bilder gesehen zu werden: Drei Fallstudien zur Methode der Interpretation altorientalischer Bilder*, Orbis Biblicus et Orientalis 112. Fribourg: Universitätsverlag. Göttingen: Vandenhoeck & Ruprecht.
Keel 1992b	Keel, O., "Iconography and the Bible, *Anchor Bible Dictionary*, vol. 3, D. N. Freedman (ed.), 6 vols. New York: Doubleday, pp. 357–374.
Keel 1998	Keel, O.,*Goddesses and Trees, New Moon and Yahweh: Ancient Near Eastern Art and the Hebrew Bible*, Journal for the Study of the Old Testament Supplement 261, Sheffield: Sheffield Academic Press.
Keel and Uehlinger 1998	Keel, O., Uehlinger, C., *Gods, Goddesses, and Images of God in Ancient Israel*, (T. H. Trapp, trans. from German), Minneapolis: Fortress.
Kelso and Thorley 1943	Kelso, J. L., Thorley, J. P., "The Potter's Technique at Tell Beit Mirsim, Particularly in Stratum A," in *The Excavation of Tell Beit Mirsim*, Vol. 3: *The Iron Age*, W. F. Albright (ed.), Annual of the American Schools of Oriental Research 21-22. New Haven: American Schools of Oriental Research, pp. 86–142.
Kletter 2010a	Kletter, R.,"The Function of Cult Stands," in *Yavneh* I, pp. 174–191.
Kletter 2010b	Kletter, R., "The Typology of the Cult Stands," in *Yavneh* I, pp, 25–45.
Kletter and Ziffer 2010	Kletter, R., Ziffer, I., "Catalogue 1: The Cult Stands," in *Yavneh* I, pp. 211–260.

Kuehni 2012 · Kuehni, R. G., "On the Relationship between Wavelength and Perceived Hue," *Color Research and Application* 37, pp. 424–428.

Kuijt and Chesson 2005 · Kuijt, I., Chesson, M. S., "Lumps of Clay and Pieces of Stone: Ambiguity, Bodies, and Identity as Portrayed in Neolithic Figurines," in *Archaeologies of the Middle East: Critical Perpsectives*, S. Pollock, R. Bernbeck (eds.), Malden, MA: Blackwell, pp. 152–183.

LeMon 2010 · LeMon, J. M., "Iconographic Approaches: The Iconic Structure of Psalm 17," in *Method Matters: Essays on the Interpretation of the Hebrew Bible in Honor of David L. Petersen*, J. M. LeMon, K. H. Richards (eds.), Leiden: Brill, pp. 143–168.

Lewis 2005 · Lewis, T. J., "Syro-Palestinian Iconography and Divine Images," in *Cult Image and Divine Representation in the Ancient Near East*, N. H. Walls (ed.), Boston: American Schools of Oriental Research, pp. 69–108.

Maeir and Dayagi-Mendels 2007 · Maeir, A. M., Dayagi-Mendels, M., "An Elaborately Decorated Clay Model Shrine from the Moussaeiff Collection," in *Bilder als Quellen,* pp. 111–123.

Mamassian 2008 · Mamassian, P., "Ambiguities and Conventions in the Perception of Visual Art," *Vision Research* 48, pp. 2143–2153.

Mastin 2004 · Mastin, B. A., "Yahweh's Asherah, Inclusive Monotheism and the Question of Dating," in *In Search of Pre–Exilic Israel*, J. Day (ed.) London: Continuum, pp. 326–351.

Maul 1994 · Maul, S. M., *Zukunftsbewältigung: Eine Untersuchung altorientalischen Denkens anhand der babylonisch-assyrischen Löserituale (Namburbi)*, Mainz am Rhein: Philipp von Zabern

Mylonas Shear 1999 · Mylonas Shear, I., "Maidens in Greek Architecture: The Origin of the 'Caryatids'," *Bulletin de Correspondance Héllenique* 123, pp. 65–85.

Nevling Porter 2003 · Nevling Porter, B., *Trees, Kings, and Politic: Studies in Assyrian Iconography*, Orbis Biblicus et Orientalis 197, Fribourg: Academic Press. Göttingen: Vandenhoeck & Ruprecht.

Niwiński 2000 · Niwiński, A., "Iconography of the 21st Dynasty: Its Main Features, Levels of Attestation, the Media, and Their Diffusion," in *Images as Media,* pp. 21–43.

Olyan 1988 · Olyan, S. M., *Asherah and the Cult of Yahweh in Israel*, Society of Biblical Literature Monograph Series 34. Atlanta: Scholars Press.

von Oppenheim 1931 · Oppenheim, M. F. von, *Der Tell Halaf: eine neue Kultur im ältesten Mesopotamien*, Leipzig, Germany: Brockhaus.

Panitz-Cohen 2010 · Panitz-Cohen, N., "The Pottery Assemblage," in *Yavneh* I, pp. 110–145.

Petty 2006 · Petty, A., *Bronze Age Anthropomorphic Figurines from Umm el–Marra, Syria: Chronology, Visual Analysis, and Function*, British Archaeological Reports 1575. Oxford: Archaeopress.

Press 2012 · Press, M. D., *Ashkelon 4: The Iron Age Figurines of Ashkelon and Philistia*, Winona Lake, Ind.: Eisenbrauns.

Reedy and Reedy 1994 · Reedy, C. L., Reedy, T. J., "Relating Visual and Technological Styles in Tibetan Sculpture Analysis," *World Archaeology* 25, pp. 304–320.

Ritner 1993 · Ritner, R. K., *The Mechanics of Ancient Egyptian Magical Practice*, Studies in Ancient Oriental Civilization 54. Chicago: Oriental Institute of the University of Chicago.

Robins 1993 · Robins, G., *Women in Ancient Egypt*, Cambridge: Harvard.

Robins 2008 · Robins, G., *The Art of Ancient Egypt*, (rev. ed.) Cambridge: Harvard University Press.

Rowe 1940 · Rowe, A., *The Four Canaanite Temples of Beth-Shan Part* 1: *The Temples and Cult Objects*, Publications of the Palestine Section of the University Museum, University of Pennsylvania 2. Philadelphia: University Museum, University of Pennsylvania Press.

Schroer 2007 · Schroer, S., "Frauenkörper als architektonische Elemente: Zum Hintergrund von Ps 144,12," in *Bilder als Quellen,* pp. 425–450.

Scurlock 2002 · Scurlock, J., "Translating Transfers in Ancient Mesopotamia," in *Magic and Ritual in the Ancient World*, P. Mirecki, M. Meyer (eds.), Religions in the Graeco–Roman World 141. Leiden: Brill, pp. 209–223.

Smith 2009 · Smith, J. S. *Art and Society in Cyprus From the Bronze Age into the Iron Age*, Cambridge: Cambridge University Press.

Smith 2002	Smith, M. S., *The Early History of God: Yahweh and the Other Deities in Ancient Israel*, Grand Rapids, Mich.: Eerdmans.
Stark 1998	Stark, M. T., "Technical Choices and Social Boundaries in Material Culture Patterning: An Introduction," in *The Archaeology of Social Boundaries*, M. T. Stark (ed.), Washington D.C.: Smithsonian, pp. 1–11.
Staubli 2009	Staubli, T., "'Den Namen Setzen': Namens-und Göttinnenstandarten in der Südlevante während der 18 ägyptischen Dynastie," in *Iconography and Biblical Studies,* pp. 93–112.
Tigay 1996	Tigay, Jefferey H., *Deuteronomy: The Traditional Hebrew Text with the New JPS Translation*, JPS Torah Commentary. Philadelphia: Jewish Publication Society.
Uehlinger 1997	Uehlinger, C., "Anthropomorphic Cult Statuary in Iron Age Palestine and the Search for Yahweh's Cult Images," in *The Image and the Book: Iconic Cults, Aniconism, and the Rise of Book Religion in Israel and the Ancient Near East*, K. van der Toorn (ed.), Contributions to Biblical Exegesis and Theology 21. Leuven: Peeters, pp. 97–155.
Weinberg 1965	Weinberg, S. S., "Ceramics and the Supernatural: Cult and Evidence in the Aegean World," in *Ceramics and Man*, F. R. Matson (ed.), Viking Fund Publications in Anthropology 41. New York: Wenner-Gren Foundation for Anthropological Research Inc., pp. 187–201.
Weissenrieder 2009	Weissenrieder, A., "The Crown of Thorns: Iconographic Approaches and the New Testament," in *Iconography and Biblical Studies*, pp. 113–138.
Wiggins 2007	Wiggins, S. A., *A Reassessment of Asherah: With Further Considerations of the Goddess*, Gorgias Ugaritic Studies 2. Piscataway, N. J.: Gorgias Press.
Winter 2010a	Winter, I. J., "Le Palais Imaginaire: Scale and Meaning in the Iconography of Neo-Assyrian Cylinder Seals," in *On Art in the Ancient Near East*, 1: *Of the First Millennium B.C.* Culture and History of the Ancient Near East 34.1. Reprinted Leiden: Brill, pp. 109–162.
Winter 2010b	Winter, I. J., "Perspective on the 'Local Style' of Hasanlu IVB: A Study in Receptivity," in *On Art in the Ancient Near East*, Volume 1: *Of the First Millennium B.C.,* Culture and History of the Ancient Near East 34.1. Reprinted Leiden: Brill, pp. 33–66.
Winter 2010c	Winter, I. J., "The Affective Properties of Style: An Inquiry into Analytical Process and the Inscription of Meaning in Art History," in *On Art in the Ancient Near East*, Volume 2: *From the Third Millennium B. C. E.*, Culture and History of the Ancient Near East 34.2. Reprinted Leiden: Brill, pp. 405–432.
Wobst 1999	Wobst, M. H., "Style in Archaeology or Archaeologists in Style," in *Material Meanings: Critical Approaches to the Interpretation of Material Culture*, E. Chilton (ed.), Salt Lake City, Utah: University of Utah Press, pp. 118–132.
Yavneh I	*Yavneh I: The Excavation of the 'Temple Hill' Repository Pit and the Cult Stands,* R. Kletter et al (eds.), Orbis Biblicus et Orientalis Series Archaeologica 30, Fribourg: Academic Press, Göttingen: Vandenhoeck & Ruprecht.
Woolley 1955	Woolley, C. L., *Alalakh: An Account of the Excavations at Tell Atchana in the Hatay, 1937–1949*, Reports of the Research Committee of the Society of Antiquaries of London 18, Oxford: Oxford University Press.
Yu 2012	Yu, X., "Exploring Visual Perception and Children's Interpretations of Picture Books," *Library and Information Science Research* 34, pp. 292–299.
Zevit 2001	Zevit, Z., *The Religions of Ancient Israel: A Synthesis of Parallactic Approaches*, London: Continuum.
Ziffer 2010	Ziffer, I., "The Iconography of the Cult Stands," in *Yavneh* I, pp. 61–104.

ERIN DARBY
University of Tennessee, Knoxville
edarby1@utk.edu

DOUBLE FACE, MULTIPLE MEANINGS
THE HELLENISTIC PILLAR FIGURINES FROM MARESHA
Adi Erlich

ABSTRACT

Maresha was a major city in Idumea during the Hellenistic period, with a mixed population of Idumeans, Sidonians, Greeks, and others. Many figurines were found in the earth fills of the numerous caves at the site, which appear to have been associated with houses above ground. This paper deals with a type found at Maresh referred to as a Hellenistic pillar figurine. The type comprises a hollow pillar with a rounded or pointed top, non-modeled backs, and plinth bases. They all portray a few types of mold-made faces, either singly or in identical pairs. These unique figurines represent a mixture of traditions: a face-type that is Eastern or Hellenistic, a body-type that recalls the Greek herm, and an overall conception rooted in the region. The Hellenistic pillar figurines make up a unique local group of terracottas, so far unknown outside Maresha and its vicinity. They present a reduction of the anthropomorphic depiction into one component, the face. A similar approach is also evident in other cultures in the region, such as the Nabatean, which generally preferred steles over figurative sculptures for the representations of their deities. The pillar figurines from Maresha illustrate the vagueness of religious iconography in the Hellenistic East.

The ancient city of Maresha (Marisa, Tel Sandahanna) in Israel, located in the Judean foothills, was a major town in the region of Idumea during the Persian and Hellenistic periods (Fig. 1). During the Hellenistic period Maresha was a bilingual town, using Greek and Aramaic simultaneously, and displaying a blend of cultures with a main Idumean identity.[1] Maresha flourished under Ptolemaic, and later Seleucid, rule. The city's life came to an end in the Hasmonean conquest of the late 2nd century B.C., when the local Idumeans were subdued by the Hasmoneans.

Excavations conducted during the course of the 20th century have yielded architectural and small finds dating to the Iron Age II, the Persian, and mainly the Hellenistic periods.[2] Since the mid-1980s the excavations have been conducted on behalf of the Israel Antiquities Authority by Amos Kloner (1985–2001) and Ian Stern and Bernie Alpert of the Archaeological Seminars (2001–present). The site consists of a tel surrounded by a lower city of approximately 80 acres. The recent excavations at the site concentrated mostly in the lower city surrounding Tel Maresha, uncovering houses,

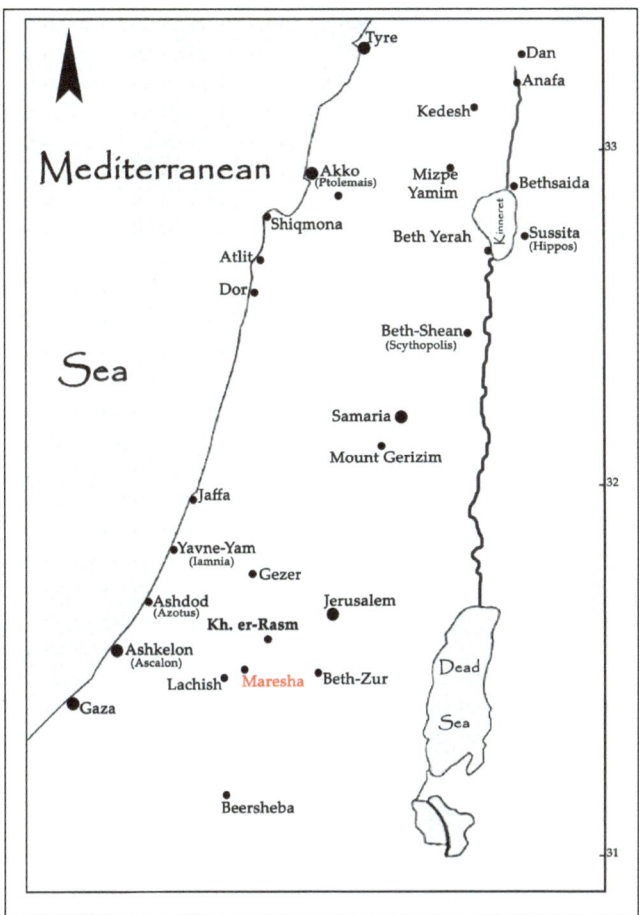

Fig. 1. Map of Hellenistic Palestine, drawn by Silvia Krapiwko.

streets, fortifications and other structures, as well as numerous rock-cut subterranean complexes, consisting of halls, cisterns, columbaria, oil presses, stables, quarries, and tombs.[3]

An outstanding feature of Maresha is its abundance of finds, mostly from the 2nd B.C., including hundreds of terracotta figurines that date from the 5th to the 2nd centuries B.C.[4] The figurines were primarily found in the earth fills of the numerous subterranean complexes at the site, while others were found in above-ground excavation areas, mostly in domestic contexts or shops. Those from the subterranean complexes also appear to have been associated with a residential neighborhood above. The overwhelming majority of the terracottas was manufactured in the city or its vicinity, as

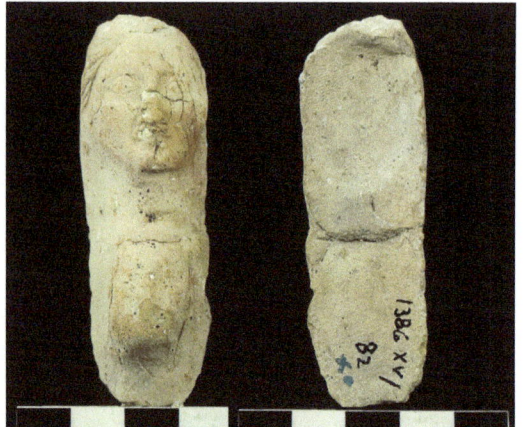

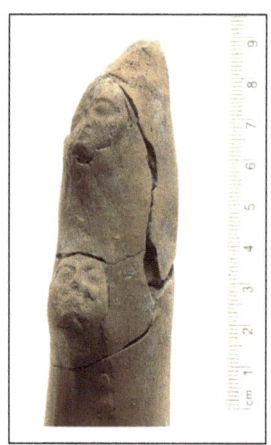

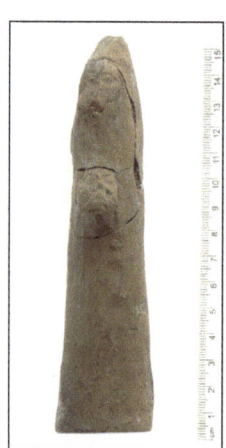

Fig. 2. (Left) Attachment of the faces of a pillar figurine from cave 75 at Maresha. Courtesy of Amos Kloner (Israel Antiquities Authority) Photo: Paul Jacobs.

Fig. 3. (Center) Attachment of the faces to a pillar figurine from cave 169 at Maresha. Courtesy of Ian Stern and Bernie Alpert (Archaeological Seminars). Photo: Clara Amit.

Fig. 4. (Right) Complete pillar figurine from cave 169. As in Fig. 3.

is attested by the appearance of the clay, petrographic analyses, and the discovery on site of molds and sets of figurines made in the same molds.[5]

Generally speaking, the Persian-period types of terracottas are typical of southern Palestinian figurines of the period, and represent the local coroplastic craft of Idumea.[6] The types of the Hellenistic period are those belonging mostly to the Eastern–Hellenistic koine, with some regional and local characteristics.[7] Among the standard types, there is a unique type of figurine that appeared in the transition of the Persian to the Early Hellenistic period and is not known outside of Maresha or its vicinity. This endemic type, which I call Hellenistic pillar figurine, and its possible meaning is the focus of this paper.

THE HELLENISTIC PILLAR FIGURINE TYPE AND ITS DATE
Technique and Typology
The type of Hellenistic pillar figurine under discus-

sion comprises a hollow pillar or peg with a rounded or pointed top, non-modeled back, and plinth base. All examples carry various types of mold-made faces, either singly, but more commonly in identical pairs, one below the other. The technique of manufacture involves several stages. First, each one of the two faces was cast in the same mold, and then the two were attached to a band of clay in a vertical alignment; the band was smoothed to blur the place of attachment, as shown in Figs. 2 and 3. The band was then attached to the upper half of the pillar, normally leaving the lower part bare. The unmodeled back was then attached to the front, usually resulting in a hollow base and solid top. The figurines stand steadily on a small plinth base and also can be easily grasped by hand. The height of the pillars is 10 to 15 cm, as shown by one complete specimen (Fig. 4). Several dozen pillar figurines of this type were unearthed at Maresha in different areas and caves, some of which were published in the report of the Hellenistic figurines from Maresha.[8]

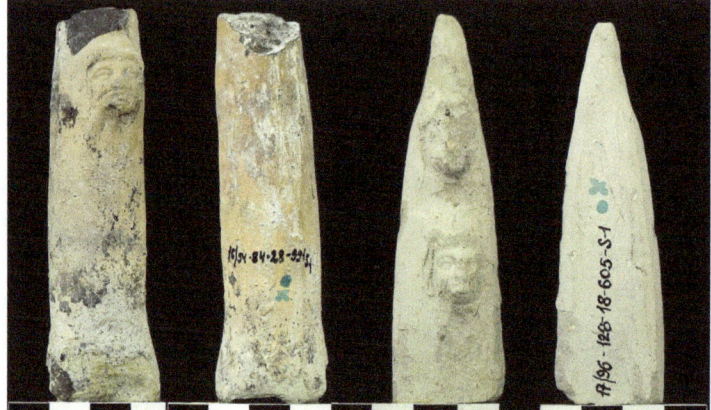

Fig. 5. Pillar figurines from Maresha, caves 84 and 128, Face type 1. Courtesy of Amos Kloner (Israel Antiquities Authority). Photo: Paul Jacobs.

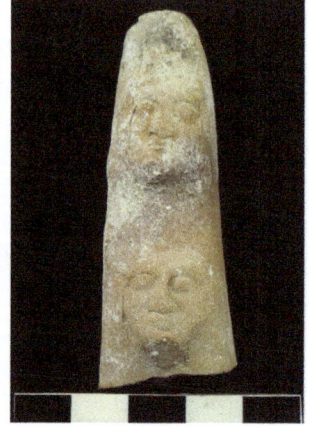

Fig. 6. Pillar figurine from cave 84 at Maresha, face type 2. Courtesy of Amos Kloner (Israel Antiquities Authority). Photo: Paul Jacobs.

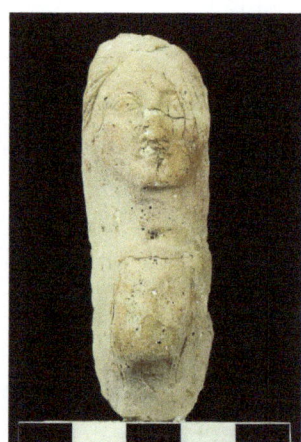

Fig. 7. Pillar figurine from cave 75 at Maresha, face type 3. Courtesy of Amos Kloner (Israel Antiquities Authority). Photo: Paul Jacobs.

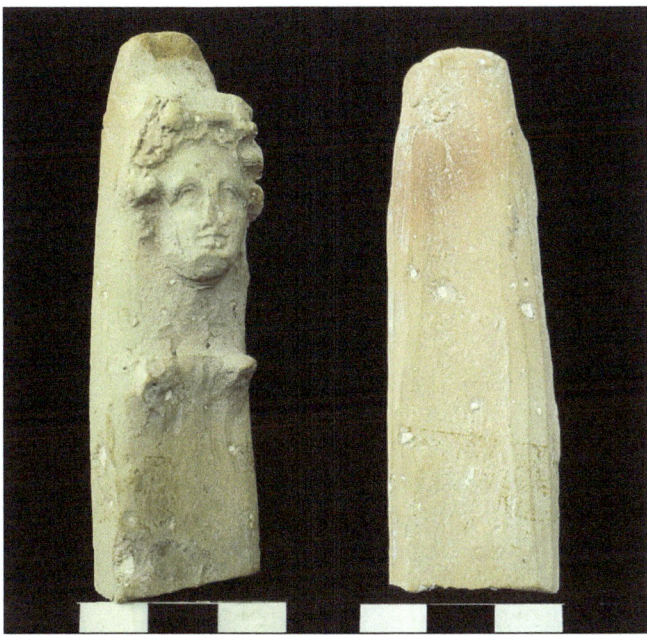

Fig. 8. Pillar figurine from cave 75 at Maresha, face type 4, Dionysos face. Courtesy of Amos Kloner (Israel Antiquities Authority). Photo: Paul Jacobs.

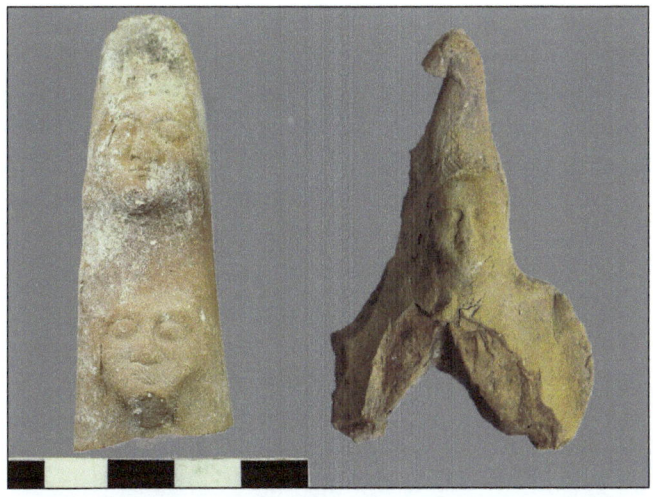

Fig. 10. (Left). Pillar figurine from cave 84 at Maresha (left), and a Persian rider on a horse from cave 169 at Maresha (right). Courtesy of Amos Kloner (Israel Antiquities Authority) and Ian Stern and Bernie Alpert (Archaeological Seminars). Photo: Paul Jacobs and Adi Erlich

This group can be divided into subtypes, according to the facial types, of which some are feminine and others male. The first subtype has two identical faces marked by narrow eyes below heavy eyelids and a low forehead covered with a band (Fig. 5). The second type is also of a double face, but is different from the first by wide-open eyes and a thick, flat nose (Fig. 6). The third type of face is similar to the previous, but it has a Cnidian hairdo, indicating its female gender (Fig. 7).

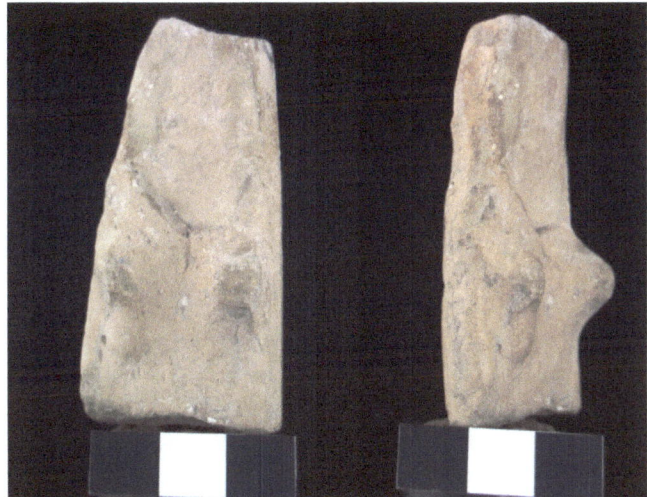

Fig. 9. Pillar figurine with two breasts from Tel Halif. Courtesy of Paul Jacobs. Photo: Paul Jacobs.

The fourth type is an unusual pillar figurine with only one face—a fine, elongated Dionysos face crowned with a typical ivy wreath on a fillet (taenia) and abundant hair similar to Hellenistic terracottas depicting Dionysos from Susa.[9] Below the face is a hand-modeled pair of schematic breasts (Fig. 8). The mixture of male and female in one body is not surprising considering the effeminacy or bisexuality of Dionysos.[10] Nevertheless, the combination of a face bearing a male identity and feminine breasts is untypical of the iconography of the deity and therefore it may indicate that the coroplast did not intend to portray Dionysos himself. Rather, he used a randomly available mold for the face, which he actually intended to look feminine, and added the breasts. As Dionysos usually had a somewhat feminine appearance in Hellenistic art, such a mold served the artist's purpose. It is uncertain how acquainted were the inhabitants of a remote, small town in the periphery of the Hellenistic world with Greek ideas of transgender and bisexuality related to Dionysos, not to say applying them to a local type by modifying it with breasts. It is therefore reasonable to interpret the Dionysos pillar with breasts as a misunderstanding or misuse of the Dionysos mold and adapting it to a local type of a pillar figurine, rather than an intended sophisticated bisexual representation of Dionysos.

The Date of the Pillar Figurines
As mentioned above, the pillar figurines were discovered throughout the site, mostly in the fills of the subterranean complexes. These fills contain finds of mostly the Persian and Hellenistic periods dated to the 5th–2nd

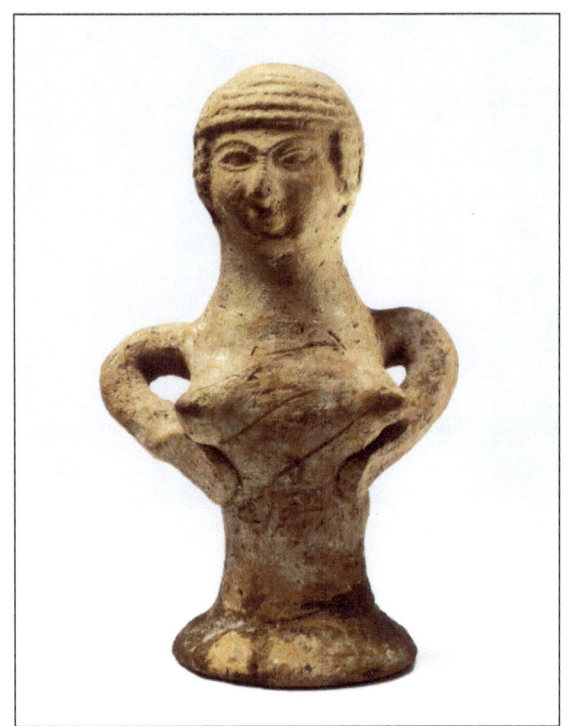

Fig. 11. Judean pillar figurine from the National Maritime Museum at Haifa. Courtesy of Avshalom Zemer. After Zemer 2009: 68.

centuries B.C. Although in most cases the archaeological context does not provide us with a precise dating, there is enough evidence to date the origin of the type to the early days of the Hellenistic period, probably the end of the 4th century B.C.

The pillar portraying Dionysos was discovered in an occupation level in subterranean cave 75 dated to the Late Persian-Early Hellenistic periods, and the Praxitilean style of its face is typical of the Early Hellenistic period.[11] A similar example is a head from neighboring Tel Lachish.[12] This piece, cast in the same mold as the Maresha figurine, is hollow, and the surviving fragment is missing the breasts that are modeled on the Maresha piece. The figurine from Tel Lachish was discovered in an unstratified context, yet its provenience—the Solar Shrine—yielded finds from the Persian and Hellenistic periods. Another fragment of a pillar figurine with two breasts, but with its face missing, was discovered at Tel Halif south of Maresha, where the greater part of the corpus of figurines is dated to the 4th century B.C.[13] (Fig. 9). The two parallels from Tel Lachish and Tel Halif are the only parallels we know of outside of Maresha. Another fragment of a pillar base from Maresha was uncovered in a fill outside a residence at area 930 that contained Persian and Hellenistic pottery.[14] It should be noted that Persian pottery at Maresha is rare relative to the presence of Hellenistic ceramics, and therefore, the discovery of two pillar figurines in relation to Persian and Hellenistic pottery should not be seen as a mere coincidence.

Another reason to link the pillar type to the Persian period lies in a figurine of another type, the so-called Persian rider type.[15] Over 50% of the Persian period types at Maresha belong to the horse and rider of the southern Idumean type.[16] One of the riders of this type strongly resembles the face type no. 2 and was probably cast in the same mold (Fig. 10). It is plausible that Persian types continued to be produced into the early Hellenistic period, at least until the end of the 4th century B.C., if not later. The resemblance of the faces of one type of the Persian rider and one type of the pillar figurine points to the relationship between the two. This dates them to the transition between the Persian and Hellenistic periods.

Despite the Late-Persian affiliation, some of the pillar figurines are stylistically Hellenistic. The face and coiffure of the female type no. 3 are Hellenistic in style. The Dionysos head of type no. 4 is also very much Hellenized and Hellenistic in style, and has no resemblance whatsoever to any Persian types from the site. Therefore, it seems that these pillar figurines were produced as early as the Early Hellenistic period and include characteristics of both the Persian and the Hellenistic periods. They also might have been in use throughout the Hellenistic period.

THE SOURCE OF THE PILLAR TYPE AND ITS MEANING

The iconography of the pillar figurines is vague and elusive. They fit within a long tradition of Canaanite and Syrian gods, who had no clear iconography—identifiable forms, features, stances, or attributes—a stark contrast to other visual systems, such as those of the Egyptian and Greek pantheons.[17] The Semitic gods were obscure characters, usually identified with more than one consort and function.[18] It was suggested that, when dealing with the realm of the East, the discussion should not center on mythological narratives or concrete deities, but on essences and varied, recurring concepts.[19] However, some of the features in the iconography of the pillars point to a certain nature or perhaps even specific identity. The interpretation of the type and its meaning should rely on exploring similar phenomena in both cultures that are hybridized in the art of Hellenistic Maresha: the local and Greek.[20]

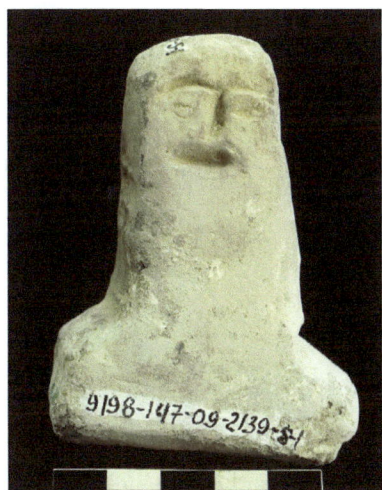

Fig. 12. Stone figurine of a herm from cave 147 at Maresha. Courtesy of Amos Kloner (Israel Antiquities Authority). Photo: Paul Jacobs.

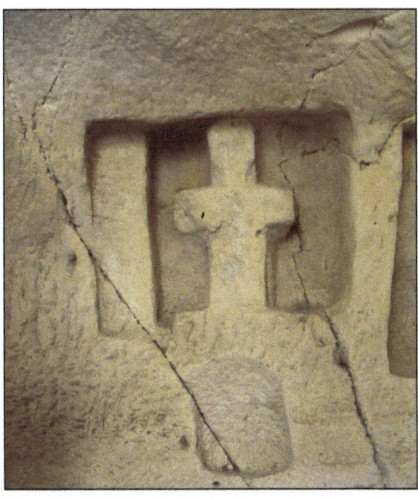

Fig. 13. Wall relief of a herm in Cave 51 at Maresha. Photo: Adi Erlich.

The Iron Age Judean Pillar Figurines

The general idea of the pillar of type 4, with its modeled breasts, can be viewed as a reminiscence of Judean pillar figurines that were widespread in Iron Age Judah.[21] The Judean pillar figurines are solid clay images that represent females supporting their breasts with their hands. The body is hand-made, rounded, pillar-like, and schematic, and the head is either mold-made or hand-made (Fig. 11). The Judean pillar figurines date to the 8th–7th centuries B.C. and their distribution is limited to areas within the borders of Judah, which in part becomes Idumea in later times. These pillar figurines have been interpreted in various ways: as Canaanite goddesses, amulets for good luck, toys, or as representations of mortal women.[22]

The Hellenistic pillars from Maresha and the Iron Age pillars from Judea share a key element—the reduction of the anthropomorphic depiction into one or two components, the head and breasts. However, there is no direct relationship between the two groups. First, the pillars of the two groups look different, as the Iron Age pillars are cylindrical whereas the Hellenistic pillars are thin and rectangular. Second, most of the Hellenistic pillars from Maresha have no breasts, and the one that does have breasts does not hold them. Third, the Iron Age figurines have only one head, while many of the Hellenistic pillars have two faces, one above the other. Fourth and last, one should bear in mind that despite the partial geographical overlapping of the two types, the Iron Age and the Hellenistic pillars are divided by some three centuries and historical and cultural chang-

es such as the Judean exile and the formation of Idumea. Therefore, it seems that although the Hellenistic pillar types may have been a late successor of the Iron Age pillars, they differ tremendously and should be treated as separate phenomena.

The Greek Herm

The general form of the pillar figurine invokes queries as to its association with Greek herms. The Dionysos head of type 4 is typical of Dionysos herms[23] and the pair of faces of the other types may be associated with the houble herm type.[24] Yet, despite the double heads, other traits rule out a direct relation to the double herm pillars: the heads are molded in relief about 1–2 cm below the top, rather than sculpted as a separate unit on top of the pillar; the faces are set one above the other, rather than on the same level on both the front and back of the pillar; there are no horizontal projections below the head resembling schematic arms, and no phalli. Moreover, double herms are rare in terracottas, due to the tendency to leave the back unmodeled. Consequently, although the outline of the Maresha pillar figurines resembles that of the Greek herm, it does not derive directly from it.

However, the herm as a sculptural form is not unfamiliar to Maresha. One terracotta from the site represents a mantle herm,[25] and herms appear in soft–limestone and on wall reliefs in some of the caves.[26] One small, schematic figurine from Maresha depicts a rectangular body on a wide rectangular base with incised facial features (Fig. 12). Among the reliefs on the walls of the underground chambers of Maresha are cruciform figures, one of which is carved as a large cross with short branches within a square depression, and its head has a schematic nose between two shallow depressions representing eyes and cheeks (Fig. 13) In an underground complex located roughly three kilometers north of Maresha was found an additional cross bearing a head and with a depression at the base of the vertical branch. These crosses can be interpreted as schematic herms, including both the pillar and the arms, but without a detailing of the face. Like the pillar figurines, some of these presentations are also uncanonical, and possibly had connections to the pillar figurines. But the many variations of this form at Maresha, in terracotta as well as in stone, attest to a rather local tradition that may have been assimilated with the Greek form.

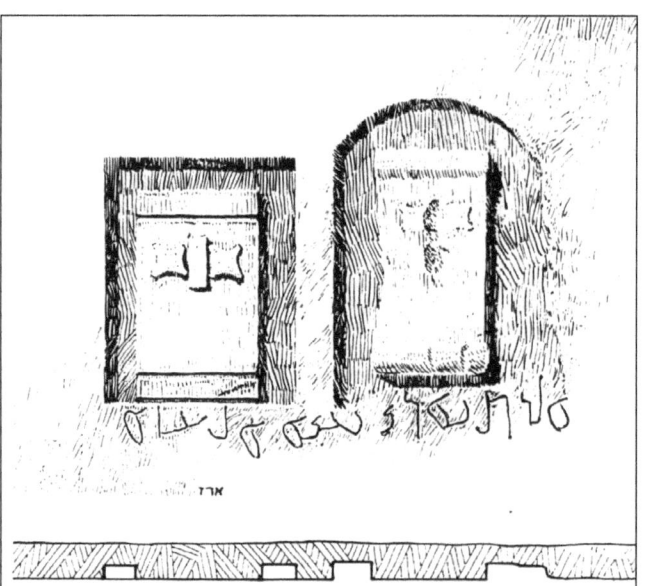

Fig. 14. Reliefs of Nabatean Eye Idols dedicated to al–Uzza and al-Kutba from Ain Shellaleh, er-Ramm. After Patrich 1990, ill.

Although the Nabatean eye idols differ from the Hellenistic pillar figurines in their shape and modeling, they share the reduction of the human body to a face, and the pairing of deities in some cases. The Nabatean steles and figurines are probably slightly later than the Maresha figurines, as most probably date to the 1st century B.C.–1st century C.E.[31] The eye idols are identified with Nabataen goddesses (al-Uzza, al-Kutba) when accompanied by inscriptions,[32] but there is not one defined scheme of correlation between the image and its identification, or in Patrich's words, "The process of creating binding cultic formulas never reached a final stage in Nabatean society. In such an evolutionary situation, it is not surprising that we can not find any clear one-to-one relationship between the stele and the god."[33] It seems that despite the small gap in time and space, i.e. Hellenistic Idumea versus early Roman Nabatea, the same can be said about the enigmatic unidentified Hellenistic pillar figurines from Maresha.

Pair, Couple or Twins?
The meaning of a pair of identical faces modeled on a single pillar is unclear; the faces may have represented two different aspects or natures of the same image or two separate figures forming a syncretic entity. One of the enduring features throughout the Hellenistic period is the divine family, which could consist of a pair of consort gods; consort gods and their child; or a mother god and her child.[34] Such combinations are evident in inscriptions from Hellenistic Palestine.[35] The double-faced pillar figurines may represent the same thing as the inscriptions dedicated to two divine entities, such as Hadad and Atargatis in an inscription from Kfar Yassif near Akko,[36] or Serapis and Isis in an inscription from Samaria.[37] Nonetheless, if the pillars were meant to represent two different deities, we would have expected the two entities to stand side by side as in the Nabatean pairs of steles, or at least to have a different appearance, unlike the sole pillar carrying two identical faces. That leads us to believe that the faces portrayed on the pillars are not two separate figures, but rather a combined entity or two very close individuals.

It seems as though the Maresha herms are not related in content to the semi-anthropomorphic herm in its various Greek forms, but to the idea of the abstraction and the minimizing of the anthropomorphic element, a trend characteristic of the region. The pillar figurines convey the same idea. They resemble the Maresha herms in their abstraction of the body and in their being a standing pillar carrying a face. However, the double face of most of the figurines of this group separates the Hellenistic pillar figurines from both the Greek herm type and the Maresha local herms.

The Nabatean 'Eye Idols'
A similar phenomenon is widespread, as can be seen among the Nabatean betyls and stele gods. They also display a preference, if not an exclusive one, for the elimination or reduction of the anthropomorphic element of the god figure.[27] Given the proximity and known relations between Nabateans and Idumeans, such a similarity is not surprising. Certain types of Nabatean steles, referred to as eye idols, came in various sizes and sculptural forms (reliefs, steles, and figurines) and occasionally carried only a face or few facial features.[28] They sometimes represented female deities, as attested by their accompanying inscriptions,[29] and recall the Maresha pillar figurines that are also largely female. Like other betyls, some of the Nabatean eye idols appear in pairs and are dedicated to two different goddesses[30] (Fig. 14).

The two heads may have also represented twins, a motif carrying profound symbolism in the ancient Near East.[38] Twins occasionally appear in terracotta figurines of the ancient Near East. Twin embryos in their mother's womb, or suckling from their mother, appear on Late Bronze plaque figurines.[39] Twin riders or a riding female accompanied by twins were depicted on

Achaemenid figurines from northern Syria.[40] But these sporadic examples come from distant sites and periods. In order to set the twins motif within its context one should look back into Hellenistic Maresha.

A figurine type frequent at Maresha depicts the Dioskouroi/Dioscuri, the Greek twin gods Castor and Pollux, the sons of Zeus and Leda and brothers of Helena.[41] The Dioskouroi from Maresha display a rather rare type (Fig. 15). They are depicted as a pair of standing young men wearing a loosely hanging chlamys and their typical headdress, the pilos. A series of figurines from Amathus, Cyprus,[42] echoing the frontal pose of the standing males, constitutes the closest parallels to the Maresha Dioskouroi.

The Dioskouroi were popular deities in the East, principally in Egypt and Syria,[43] owing to their astral character, protective role, versatile tasks, and diverse identifications with local deities. Their cult was practiced in Ptolemaic Egypt and in Cyprus.[44] In Hellenistic Palestine Dioskouroi appear in other media as well.[45] They can be found on coins of the 2nd century BCE from 'Akko-Ptolemais on the north coast of Palestine.[46] A Hellenistic inscription from Scythopolis mentions the savior deities, perhaps referring to the Dioskouroi.[47] Two identical stone reliefs depicting only a pilos and star were unearthed at Samaria, within a wall of the Roman temple dedicated to Kore,[48] possibly indicating an earlier, probably Hellenistic, cult of the Dioskouroi.

The Hellenistic pillar figurines are different from the Dioskouroi terracottas in composition and sometimes also in gender. Still, it is worthwhile to point at a striking similarity between the faces of one of the Dioskouroi types at Maresha and the second face type of the pillar figurines. They both have the same wide-open eyes and flat nose. This resemblance implies that they might represent the same idea of identical, if not Siamese, twins, whether male or female. The divine twins are a long lasting motif in ancient cultures. At Egypt there were Shu and Tefenet and other divine or majestic twins, which are evident also in Graeco–Roman times.[49] The myth of twins as an astral power is evident also in the ancient Near East.[50] In the Greek world there were Castor and Pollux, mentioned above, who were the source for the sign of the Gemini in the Zodiac.[51] In Roman cultures there are of course Romulus and Remus, the founders of Rome. Often the twins were

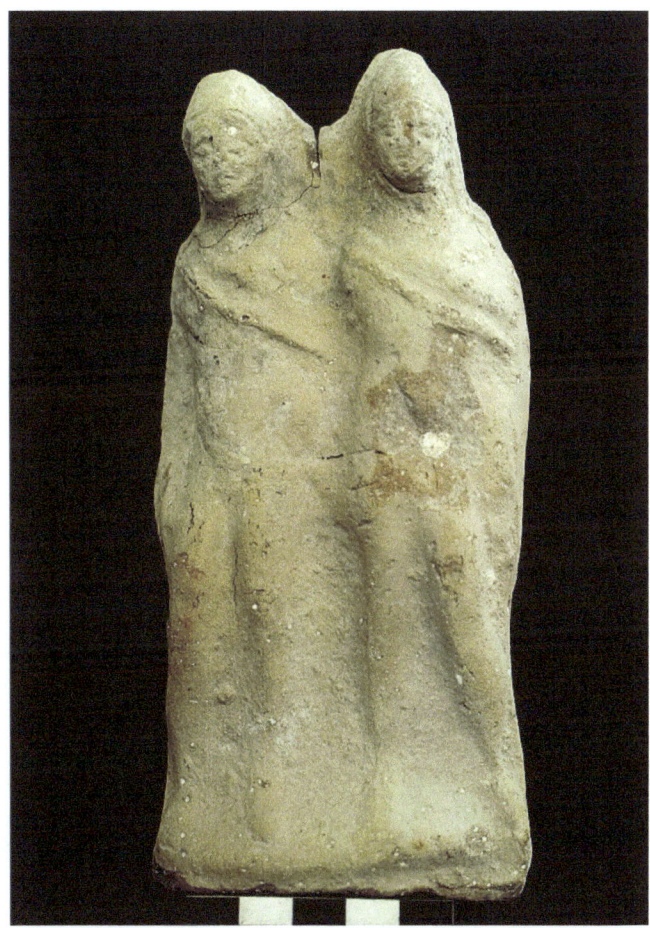

Fig. 15. Dioskouroi figurine from cave 90 at Maresha. Courtesy of Amos Kloner (Israel Antiquities Authority) and Ian Stern and Bernie Alpert (Archaeological Seminars). Photo: Paul Jacobs.

considered to be heavenly and astral, and connected to the sun and the moon or to the stars.

There is one local pair of twins which should attract our attention, the biblical Jacob and Esau, from which the people of Israel and the Edomites are said to have emerged.[52] Although the origin of the Idumeans is obscure, Idumea in the Persian and Hellenistic periods seems to be the inheritor of biblical Edom,[53] especially when considering the popularity of Edomite names at Maresha and Idumea.[54] The claim of the Idumeans for south Judea is rooted in their being the successors of Esau, the deceived and deprived elder twin who did not succeed to inherit Jacob's land.[55] The myth of the twins is interlaced in the heritage of both nations, Jews and Idumeans, after the first temple period.[56] It could be that such an ancient local concept of twins as divine astral power, or as founders of nations, is represented in the double-faced Hellenistic pillar figurines. Nevertheless, it should be noted that not all the pillars carry two faces, and one certainly carries only one Dionysos face. Therefore, the twins interpretation may be valid only in some of the cases which form the majority of the Hellenistic pillar figurines.

CONCLUSIONS

The exact meaning and function of the double faced pillar figurines from Maresha are still vague. The pillars may represent specific deities, such as Dionysos or the Dioskouroi. They are frequently female, but in certain cases also males are represented in them. They have one or, more often, two faces. They are meant to stand on a solid base, but they are also easily held in the hand. They all share the reduction of the human body to a tall slender pillar with a face. As was maintained above, they find parallels in the concept of the Greek herm, but also in the Nabatean betyls and stele gods, which also display a preference for the elimination or reduction of the anthropomorphic element of the god figure. Another key element common to the Maresha pillars and the Nabatean steles is the flexibility of iconography; they seem to be a mere platform for altering entities and identities.

The Hellenistic pillar figurines are not found outside Maresha, except for one type found in two sites south of Maresha, Tel Lachish and Tel Halif, both in the heart of Idumea. The regionalism of the Idumean figurines is not a new feature of the Hellenistic period; Idumea has featured its own regional types as early as the Persian period.[57] The pillar figurines are part of this regionalism, although many of the Hellenistic figurines from Maresha are koine types. The inhabitants of Maresha created a local form of figurine, using conventionalized molds. This form might have been divine or mortal, female or male, representing local deities or Greek divinities, related to the Dioskouroi twins or to another pair; we can not tell for sure. The pillars from Maresha are evident for a local and independent Idumean tradition.

ACKNOWLEDGMENTS

I would like to thank the excavators of Maresha who have entrusted me with the terracotta figurines from the site. I am indebted to my teacher, colleague and friend, Prof. Amos Kloner of Bar Ilan University and the Israel Antiquities Authority, who had been excavating Maresha until 2000. I would like to extend my deep gratitude to Dr. Ian Stern and Bernie Alpert of Archaeological Seminars, who have been excavating Maresha since 2001.

For his help and cooperation I am thankful to Prof. Paul Jacobs of the Mississippi State University, who studied and photographed the Tel Halif figurines and photographed the Maresha figurines. I extend my gratitude to Prof. Yosef Patrich of the Hebrew University and to Avshalom Zemer of the National Maritime Museum at Haifa for letting me use their illustrations. I also am thankful to my dear friends Benjamin Gordon, who edited this text, and Silvia Krapiwko, who prepared the photographs.

NOTES

[1] Peters and Thiersch 1905, p. 68; Oren and Rappaport 1984, pp. 142–148; Eshel 2007; Kloner et al 2010.

[2] Bliss and Macalister 1902, pp. 52-61; Kloner 2003, pp. 9–30.

[3] Kloner et al 2010, pp. 1–33, 205–216.

[4] Erlich 2006; Erlich and Kloner 2008.

[5] Erlich and Kloner 2008, pp. 113–114.

[6] Erlich 2006.

[7] Erlich 2009, pp. 51–58.

[8] Erlich and Kloner 2008, pp. 43–46, pl. 24.

[9] Martinez–Sève 2002, pp. 118–119.

[10] Jameson 1993, pp. 44–45; Stewart 1997, pp. 228.

[11] Erlich and Kloner 2008: 43–44, 95–96, 117.

[12] Aharoni 1975: Pl. 18:2.

[13] Jacobs, forthcoming.

[14] Erlich and Kloner 2008: 46, no. 137.

[15] Moorey 2000.

[16] Erlich 2006.

[17] Boardman 2000, pp. 324, 333.

[18] Cumont 1956, pp. 131–132; Moscati 1968, pp. 31–38.

[19] Keel and Uehlinger 1998, pp. 12–13, 393–394.

[20] For the syncretic nature of Hellenistic Levant see Erlich 2009, p.107; Kouremnos, Chandrasekaran and Rossi 2011.

[21] Kletter 1996; Kletter 2001. See also Darby 2013.

[22] Kletter 2001, pp. 195–201.

[23] Goldman 1942.

[24] Marcadé 1952.

[25] Erlich and Kloner 2008, pp. 60–61, pl. 36, no. 195.

[26] Erlich 2009, pp. 19–22.

[27] Patrich 1990, pp. 165–166.

[28] Ibid., pp. 82–86.

[29] Ibid., pp. 54–55, ill. 7, 62 ill. 9.

[30] Loc. cit., 62, ill. 9; Bartlett 2007, pp. 66–68.

[31] Patrich 1990, pp. 95–96.

[32] Ibid., pp. 101–106.

[33] Ibid., p. 104.

[34] Teixidor 1977, pp. 34–59.

[35] Erlich 2009, pp. 112–113.

[36] Avi-Yonah 1959.

[37] Crowfoot, Crowfoot and Kenyon 1957, p. 37, no. 13.

[38] Kuntzmann 1983.

[39] Ornan 2007.

[40] Nunn 2000, pp. 44–45, pls. 15–16; Nunn 2004, pp. 151–161, type d.

[41] Erlich and Kloner 2008, pp. 5–7, pl. 1.

[42] Queyrel 1988, pls. 25, 26.

[43] Barry 1906, pp. 168; Augé and Bellefonds 1986a, pp. 593.

[44] Fraser 1972, p. 207; Queyrel 1985; Barnard 2003.

[45] Erlich 2009, p. 22.

[46] Kadman 1961, p. 51, pl. 2; Lipinski 1995, p. 283.

[47] Ovadiah 1975.

[48] Crowfoot, Kenyon and Sukenik 1942, p. 66, pl. LX:2.

[49] Baines 1985, pp. 472–477.

[50] Kuntzmann 1983, pp. 137–163.

[51] Hermary 1986, p. 592; Fishof 2001, p. 107.

[52] *Gen.* 25, 22–34; Kuntzmann 1983, pp. 39–50.

[53] Kokkinos 1998, pp. 36–50.

[54] Stern 2007; Eshel 2007.

[55] *Gen.* 27, Kokkinos 1998, pp. 37–38.

[56] Assis 2006.

BIBLIOGRAPHY

Aharoni 1975 — Aharoni,Y., *Investigation at Lachish* V: *The Sanctuary and the Residency*, Publications of the Institute of Archaeology, Tel Aviv University 4. Tel Aviv: Gateway Publishers.

Assis 2006 — Assis, E., "Why Edom? On the Hostility towards Jacob's Brother in Prophetic Sources," *Vetus Testamentum* 56, pp. 1–20.

Augé and linant de Bellefonds 1986	Augé, C., linant de Bellefonds, P., "Dioskouroi in periphria orientali," *Lexicon Iconographicum Mythologicae Classicae,* Zurich & Munich III, pp. 593–597.
Avi-Yonah 1959	Avi-Yonah, M., "Syrian Gods of Ptolemais-Accho," *Israel Exploration Journal* 9, pp. 1–12.
Baines 1985	Baines, J. R. , "Egyptian Twins," *Orientalia* 54, pp. 461–482.
Barnard 2003	Barnard, S., "The Dioscuri on Cyprus," *Thetis* 10, pp. 71–75.
Barry 1906	Barry, M. L., "Sur une lampe en terre cuite. Le culte de Tyndarides dans l'Égypte gréco–romaine," *Bulletin de l'institut Français d'archéologie orientale de Caire* 5, pp. 165–181.
Bartlett 2007	Bartlett, J. R., "Nabataean Religion," in *The World of the Nabataeans*, Volume 2 of the International Conference The World of the Herods and the Nabataeans Held at the British Museum (17 April–19 April 2001), K. D. Politis (ed.), Stuttgart: Franz Steiner Verlag, p. 55–78.
Bliss and Macalister 1902	Bliss, F. G. and Macalister R. A. S., *Excavations in Palestine during the Years 1898–1900*, London: Palestine Exploration Fund.
Boardman 2000	Boardman, J., "Images and Media in the Greek World," in *Images as Media,* pp. 323–337.
Crowfoot, Crowfoot, and Kenyon 1957	Crowfoot, J. W., Crowfoot, G. M., and Kenyon, K. M., *Samaria-Sebastie* III: *The Objects from Samaria*, London: Palestine Exploration Fund.
Crowfoot, Kenyon and Sukenik 1942	Crowfoot, J.W., Kenyon, K.E., and Sukenik, E.L., *The Buildings at Samaria*, London: Palestine Exploration Fund.
Cumont 1956	Cumont, F. V. M., *The Oriental Religions in Roman Paganism*, New York: Dover Publications.
Darby 2013	Darby, E. D., "Seeing Double: Viewing and Re-viewing Judean Pillar Figurines through Modern Eyes," *Occasional Papers in Coroplastic Studies* 1, pp. 13–24.
Erlich 2006	Erlich, A., "The Persian Terracotta Figurines from Maresha in Idumea: Local and Regional Aspects," *Transeuphratène* 32, pp. 45–59.
Erlich 2009	Erlich, A., *The Art of Hellenistic Palestine*, BAR International Series 2010, Oxford: Archaeopress.
Erlich and Kloner 2008	Erlich, A., Kloner, A., *Maresha Excavations Final Report* II, *Hellenistic Terracotta Figurines from the 1989–1996 Seasons*. IAA Reports 35. Jerusalem: Israel Antiquities Authority.
Eshel 2007	Eshel, E., "The Onomasticon of Mareshah," in *Judah and the Judeans in the Fourth Century B.C.E.*, O. Lipschits et al (eds.), Winona Lake: Eisenbrauns, pp. 145–156.
Fishof 2001	Fishof, I., *Written in the Stars: Art and Symbolism of the Zodiac*, Jerusalem: The Israel Museum.
Fraser 1972	Fraser, P. M., *Ptolemaic Alexandria*, Oxford: Oxford University Press.
Goldman 1942	Goldman, H., "The Origin of the Greek Herm," *American Journal of Archaeology* 46, pp. 58–68.
Hermary 1986	Hermary, A., "Dioskouroi," *Lexicon Iconographicum Mythologicae Classicae*, Zurich & Munich III, pp. 567–593.
Jacobs, forthcoming	Jacobs, P., *Lahav* IV. *The Figurines of Halif*, Winona Lake: Eisenbrauns.
Jameson 1993	Jameson, M., "The Asexuality of Dionysus, in *Masks of Dionysus*, T. H. Carpenter, C. A. Faraone. (eds.), Ithaca and London: Cornell University Press, pp.44–64.
Kadman 1961	Kadman, L., *The Coins of Akko Ptolemais. Corpus Nummorum Palaestinensium* IV. Jerusalem: Schocken.
Keel and Uehlinger 1998	Keel, O., Uehlinger, C., *Gods, Goddesses and Images in Ancient Israel*. Minneapolis: Fortress Press.
Kletter 2001	Kletter, R., "Between Archaeology and Theology: The Pillar Figurines from Judah and the Asherah," in *Studies in the Archaeology of the Iron Age in Israel and Jordan,* A. Mazar (ed.), Journal for the Study of the Old Testament Supplement Series 331. Sheffield: Sheffield Academic Press, pp. 179–216.
Kloner 2003	Kloner, A., *Maresha Excavations Final Report* 1: *Subterranean Complexes 21, 44, 70.* IAA Reports 17. Jerusalem: Israel Antiquities Authority.

Kloner et al 2010 — Kloner, A. et al, *Maresha Excavations Final Report* III, *Epigraphic Finds from the 1989–2000 Seasons*, IAA Reports 45. Jerusalem: Israel Antiquities Authority.

Kokkinos 1998 — Kokkinos, N., *The Herodian Dynasty, Origins, Role in Society and Eclipse.* Journal for the Study of the Pseudepigrapha Supplement Series 30. Sheffield: Sheffield Academic Press.

Kouremnos et al 2011 — Kouremnos, A. et al, *Hybridisation and Identity in the Art and Architecture of the Hellenistic East* (BAR International Series 2221). Oxford: Archaeopress.

Kuntzmann 1983 — Kuntzmann, R., *Le symbolisme des jumeaux au Proche-Orient ancien. Naissance, fonction et évolution d'un symbole*, Paris: Beauchesne.

Lipinski, 1995 — Lipinski, E., *Dieux et déesses de l'univers phénicien et punique.* Studia Phoenicia XIV. Leuven: Peeters.

Marcadé 1952 — Marcadé, J., "Hermès doubles," *Bulletin de correspondance hellénique* 76, pp. 596–624.

Martinez–Sève 2002 — Martinez–Sève, L., *Les figurines de Suse de l'époque néo–élamite à l'époque sassanide*, Paris: Editions de la Réunion des musées nationaux.

Moorey 2000 — Moorey, P. R. S., "Iran and the West: The Case of the Terracotta 'Persian' Riders in the Achaemenid Empire," in *Variatio Delectat, Iran und der Westen, Gedenkschrift für Peter Calmeyer*, R. Dittmann et al (eds.), Münster Ugarit-Verlag, pp. 469–486.

Moscati 1968 — Moscati, S., *The World of the Phoenicians*, London: Weidenfeld and Nicolson.

Nunn 2000 — Nunn, A., *Der figürliche Motivschatz Phöniziens, Syriens, und Transjordaniens vom 6. bis zum 4. Jahrhundert v. Chr,* Orbis Biblicus et Orientalis 18. Göttingen: Vandenhoeck & Ruprecht.

Nunn 2004 — Nunn, A., "Images de déesses?," *Transeuphratène* 28, pp. 149–163.

Oren and Rappaport 1984 — Oren, E. D., Rappaport, U., "The Necropolis of Maresha-Beth Govrin," *Israel Exploration Journal* 34, pp. 114–153.

Ornan 2007 — Ornan, T., "Labor Pangs: The Revadim Plaque Type," in *Bilder als Quellen,* pp. 215–235.

Ovadiah 1975 — Ovadiah, A., "Greek Cults in Beth-Shean/Scythopolis in the Hellenistic and Roman Periods," *Eretz Israel* 12, pp. 116–124 (Hebrew; English summary, p. 122*).

Patrich 1990 — Patrich, J., *The Formation of Nabatean Art, Prohibition of a Graven Figure among the Nabateans.* Jerusalem: Magness Press.

Peters and Thiersch 1905 — Peters, J. P. and Thiersch H., *Painted Tombs in the Necropolis of Marissa*, London: Palestine Exploration Fund.

Queyrel 1985 — Queyrel, A., "Les Dioscures à Amathonte," Report of the Department of Antiquities Cyprus, pp. 320–324.

Queyrel 1988 — Queyrel, A., *Amathonte* IV, *Les figurines hellénistiques de terre cuite* (École française d'Athènes, Etudes Chypriotes, X). Paris: De Boccard.

Stern 2007 — Stern, I., "The Population of Persian-Period Idumea According to the Ostraca: A Study of Ethnic Boundaries and Ethnogenesis," in A *Time of Change, Judah and its Neighbours in the Persian and Early Hellenistic Periods*, Y. Levin (ed.), Library of Second Temple Studies 65. London: T&T Clark, pp. 205–238.

Stewart 1997 — Stewart, A., *Art, Desire and the Body in Ancient Greece*, Cambridge: Cambridge University Press.

Teixidor 1977 — Teixidor, J., *The Pagan God, Popular Religion in the Greco-Roman Near East*, Princeton: Princeton University Press.

Zemer 2009 — Zemer, A., *Terracotta Figurines in Ancient Times*, Haifa Museums, The National Maritime Museum, Winter 2009. Haifa: Haifa Museums.

ADI ERLICH
University of Haifa
aerlich@research.haifa.ac.il

THE MIMESIS OF A WORLD
THE EARLY AND MIDDLE BRONZE CLAY FIGURINES FROM EBLA-TELL MARDIKH
Marco Ramazzotti

ABSTRACT

The paper will focus on the cognitive and spatial analysis of clay figurines dated to the Early and Middle Bronze Age that were recently discovered in Ebla-Tell Mardikh (Syria). The results outline a symbolic *chaîne opératoire* of these clay artifacts and underline their ideographic and composite character, which also can be paralleled in the Early Dynastic and Early Syrian miniature statue tradition. It will then be suggested that these products of the so-called 'material culture' were also a conscious human imitation of sacred and royal images of power. It has been observed that during the Early Syrian Period (2400-2000 B.C.) the spatial concentration of clay figurines in the Royal Palace G of Ebla does not seem accidental, a likelihood that could demonstrate a sort of affinity of this miniature clay world with that of the sacred kingship. However, I would argue that even though the spatial distribution of the clay figurines from the Old Syrian Period (2000–1600 B.C.) is indeed extensive, the strong concentration of figurine fragments that was found close to the Ishtar public cult area (Monument P3 and Temple P2) seems to indicate a radical transformation of the roles played by this clay world. Rather than being a mimesis of the physical and metaphysical sacred kingship, it is instead a reproduction of the whole society.

THE EARLY SYRIAN AND OLD SYRIAN CLAY FIGURINES AT EBLA

Within the Early and Old Syrian coroplastic corpus from Ebla[1] there are a number of clay representations of the human and animal world that could be considered products of the first Mesopotamian state societies,[2] well adapted to the contextual, economic condition of the so-called northern secondary urbanism (Figs. 1a–b).[3] This specific, archetypical relationship between southern and northern Mesopotamia was strongly reinforced by the economic and political network of the Uruk Period. During the Late Uruk Period, at the end of the 4th millennium B.C., this network comprised an interchangeable continuum of materials, techniques, and images[4] that included the Sumerian technique of modeling in clay, or molding the earth, a technique that pre-dated the mechanical reproduction of figurines by means of a mold.[5] For this reason, many centuries later in the second half of the third millennium B.C., we still find at Ebla-Tell Mardikh in northern Syria a local translation of the Sumerian tradition of the miniature representation of the human and the appearance of a variety of shapes and styles contemporary with the Early Dynastic symbolic tradition. Typologically, we can distinguish these miniatures as Early Syrian from their distinctive iconographic character[6] and their similarity to many other contemporary images from north

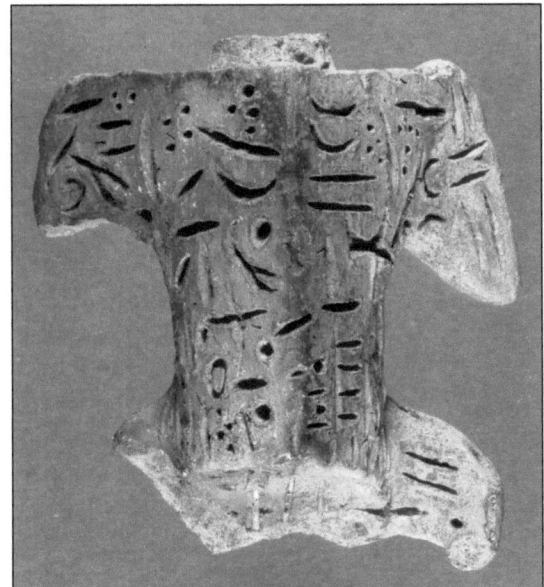
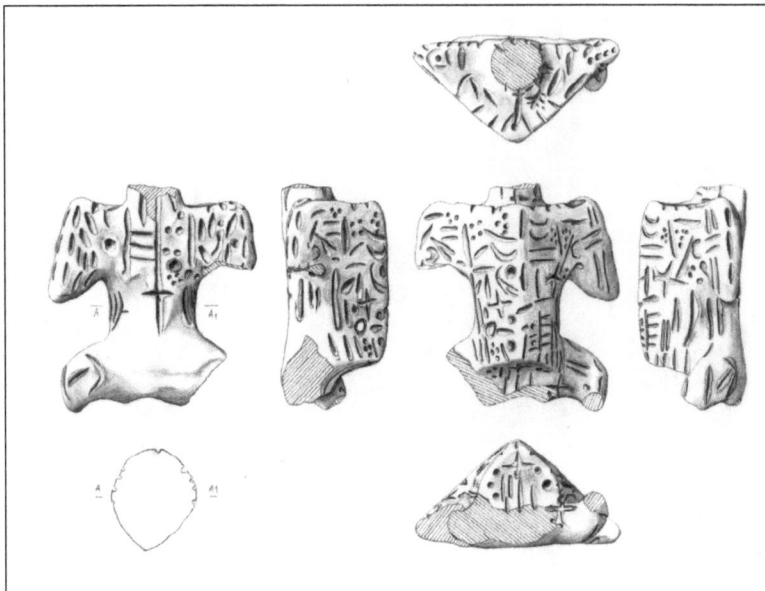

Figs. 1a–b: TM83G311 Early Syrian Clay Turtle.(© La Sapienza University of Rome – Missione Archeologica Italiana in Siria)

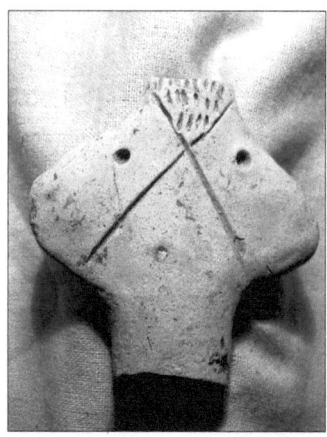
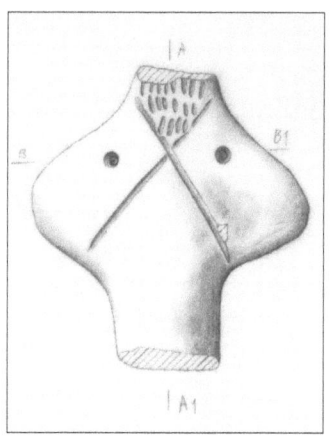
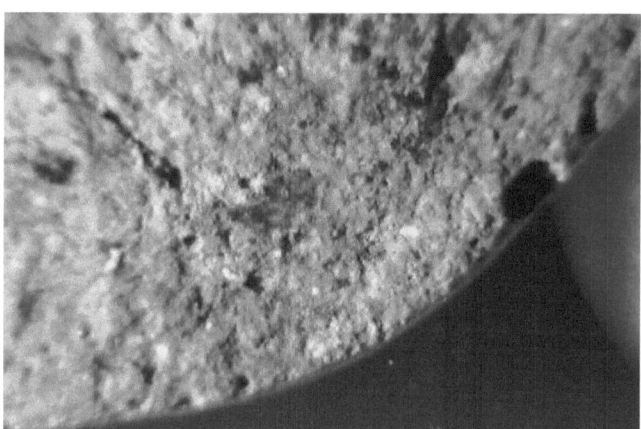

Figs. 2a–c. TM83G361 Early Syrian Clay Figurine. Photo: © La Sapienza University of Rome, Missione Archeologica Italiana in Siria)

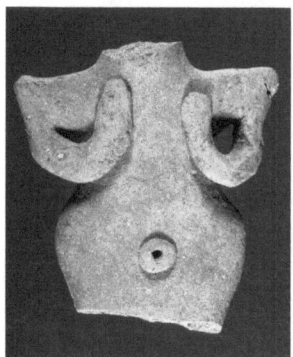
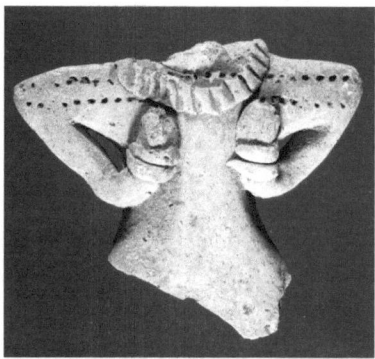

Figs. 3a–b: TM06HH0934 and TM07G174 Early Syrian Clay Figurines. Photo: © La Sapienza University of Rome, Missione Archeologica Italiana in Siria)

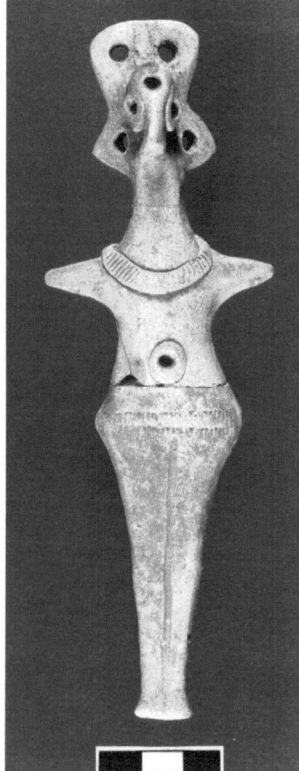
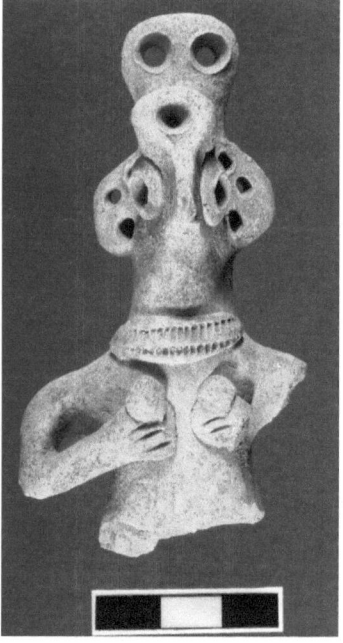

Figs. 4a–b: TM06HH0097+0738 and TM06HH0237: Old Syrian Clay Figurines. Photo: © La Sapienza University of Rome, Missione Archeologica Italiana in Siria)

Syrian urban centers (Figs. 2a–b).[7] During the Early Dynastic and the Early Syrian periods in Mesopotamia and in Syria the quantity and variability of clay figurines increased, while the hybridism recognized during the Halaf and Ubaid period[8] almost disappeared in favor of the more naturalistic representations of the Uruk/Jemdet Nasr period.[10] The exponential growth in the manufacture of clay figurines, the reduction of hybrid images, and the appearance of naturalistic representations are variables of complex phenomena probably related to the political and economic characteristics of secondary urbanization, a different replica of the Mesopotamian urban revolution (Figs. 3a–b).[10] Subsequently, the technique of agglutinated, composite, molded elements that appears on a wide variety of Early Syrian artifacts was replaced by closer imitations of the real and/or metaphysical world during the Old Babylonian and Syrian periods.[11] At this time the highly diversified Early Syrian figurines were produced in uniform series (Figs. 4a–b)[12] that were not related to only the female, male, or animal classes, but also to some specific breakages, or fractures. However, in the same period the figurines were highly structured, with the hand–modeled examples related to the divided spheres of hybrids, humans, and animals that were based on a shared model with standard proportions and dimensions (Fig. 5a–b).[13] This transformation began suddenly, probably with the collapse of Early Syrian centralized political power at the beginning of the Akkadian period, when the aggressive expansion of the Sargonic royal household, at the expense of many local institutions, is attested.[14] In this period —after the "Fall"[15] — we have some rare and unusual painted clay figurines that cannot be automatically assigned to the previous tradition.[16] In any case, from the

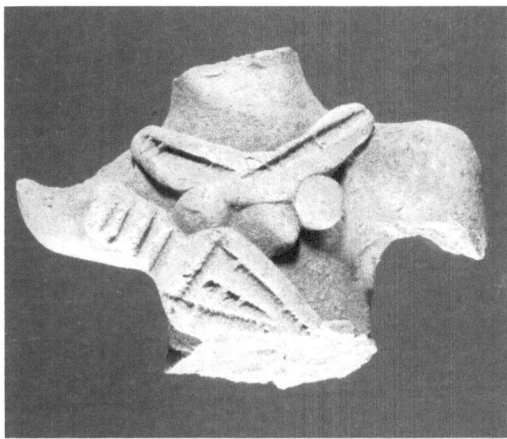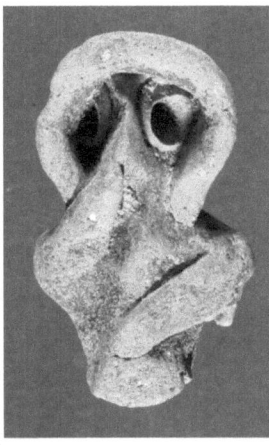

Figs. 5a–b. TM76G476 and TM94P666: Old Syrian Clay Figurines. Photo: © La Sapienza University of Rome, Missione Archeologica Italiana in Siria)

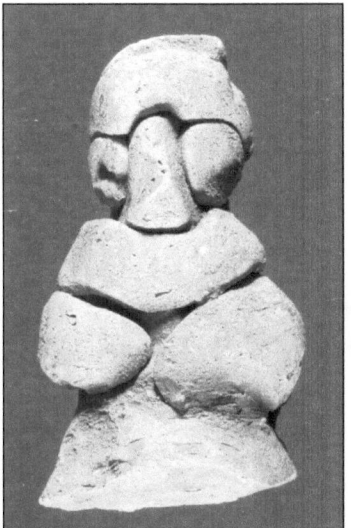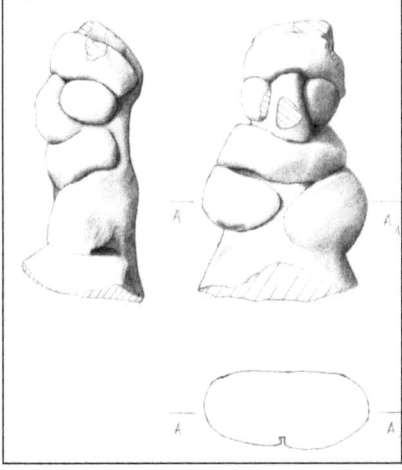

Figs. 6a–b. TM92P717 and TM06HH410: Old Syrian Clay Figurines. Photo: © La Sapienza University of Rome, Missione Archeologica Italiana in Siria.

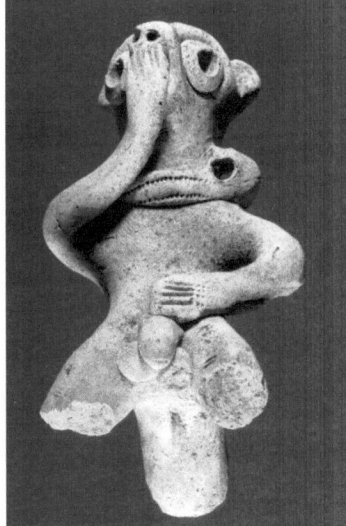

Fig. 7. TM06HH410: Old Syrian Clay Figurine. Photo: © La Sapienza University of Rome, Missione Archeologica Italiana in Siria.

beginning of the Old Syrian period onward, human, animal, and divine figures proliferated. But within the *habitus*, or social values, of this mass production the tendency to formalize more ancient schemes of representation coexisted with the tendency to maintain archaic, ideographic codes in order to make subject matter recognizable (Figs. 6a–b; Fig. 7).[17] These ideographic codes, the use of clay details on the image, and the place of the image as a socially recognizable aspect of the institutional, political, and religious roles of the represented subjects were probably inspired by popular imitation and translation of some contemporary Old Syrian works, such as the Face of Ishtar, which were impressive images of the most archaic Eblaite kingship and religious power.[18] Examples of this can be seen in clay imitations of the most archaic sacred images (Table II:A, TM83G400), such as the miniature statue in hematite, white marble, and red jasper discovered in the Royal Palace G (Table II:A, TM94P666), and reproduced—probably as a queen—in another important, but fragmentary, Early Syrian votive plaque representing a banquet scene. There are also clay reproductions of the most popular Old Syrian sacred images (Table II:B, TM88R035), such as the nude Ishtar representation in the fragmentary basalt basin from Temple P2 (TM08P2–916), or the clay imitations of archetypical symbols of kingship in the basalt monumental sculptures (TM64B35), such as the lions' heads well attested at Ebla during the Old Syrian period (TM95P260 / TM91P251). Additionally, there are the clay mimesis of ideological actions of kingship in the wooden and ivory inlays (Table II:C, TM93P340), such as the iconography of the king carrying an animal offering (Table II:C, TM92P596). Moreover, during the Late Old Syrian period we witness the multiplication of figurines that are not properly imitations and/or representations, but rather follow an autonomous composite path: theriomorphic vases, ceremonial chariots, and incense burners. These clay objects show that the clay as "matter of creation" for humans and animals and "matter of tactile mimesis" of humankind be-

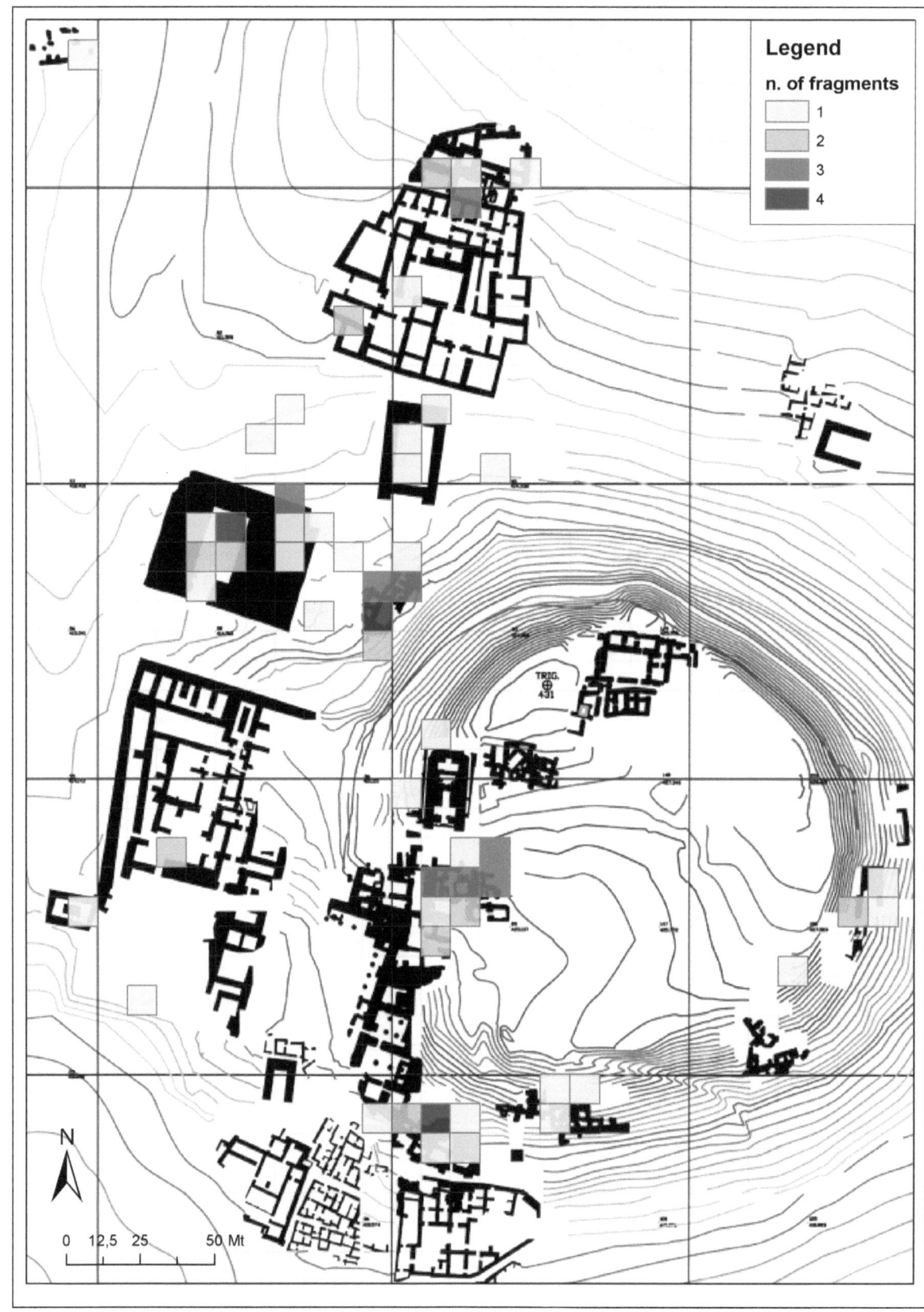

Table I:A. Spatial distribution of 100 clay figurines from Ebla dated to EB and MB period; B. Spatial distribution of 100 clay figurines main breakages (heads; chests; legs; pubes; complete); C. Spatial distribution of the 50 clay figurines Early Syrian breakages; D. Spatial distribution of the 50 clay figurines Old Syrian breakages. © La Sapienza University of Rome ARCHEOSEMA Digital Archive.

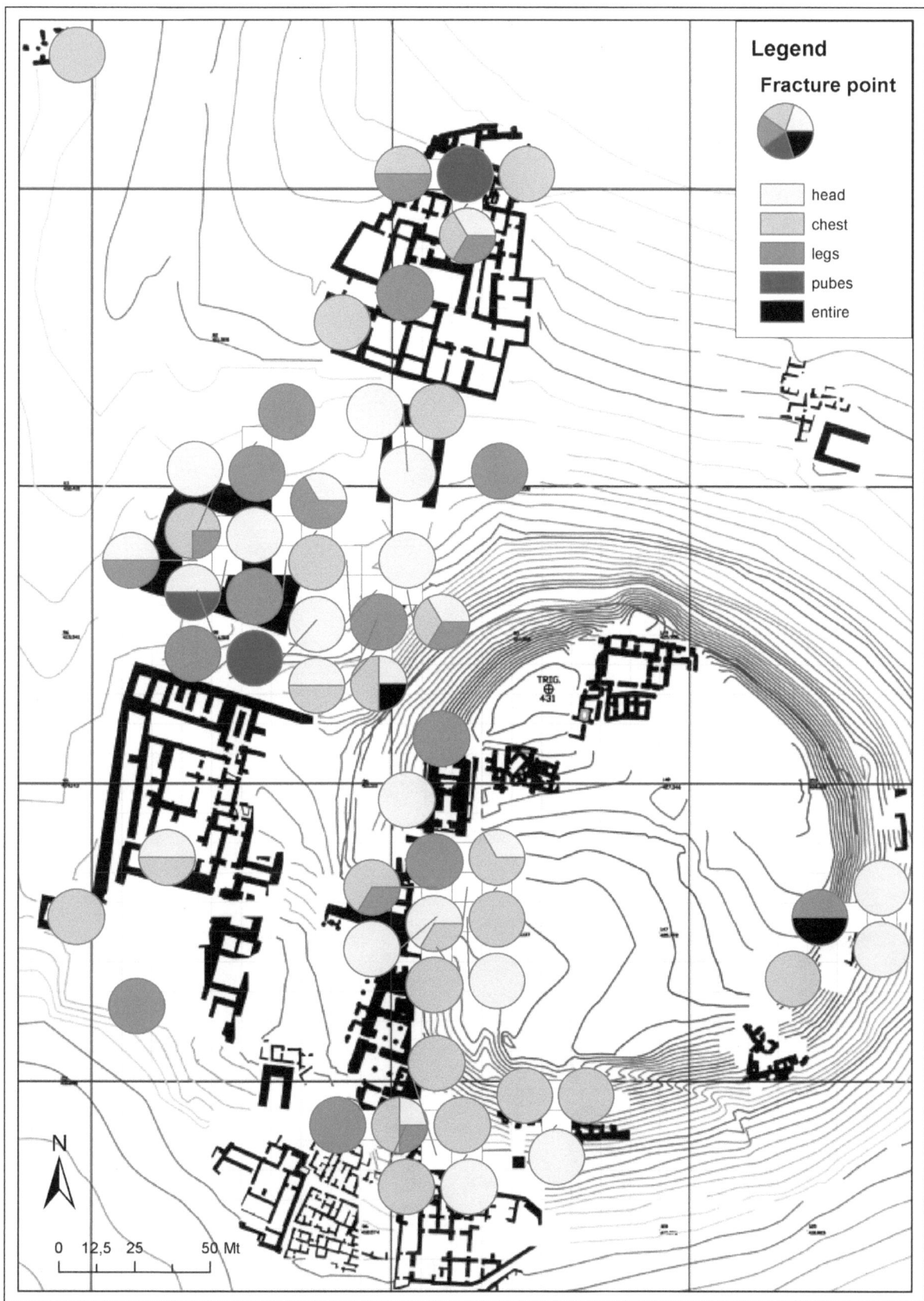

Table I:B. Spatial distribution of 100 clay figurines main breakages (heads; chests; legs; pubes; complete). © La Sapienza University of Rome ARCHEOSEMA Digital Archive.

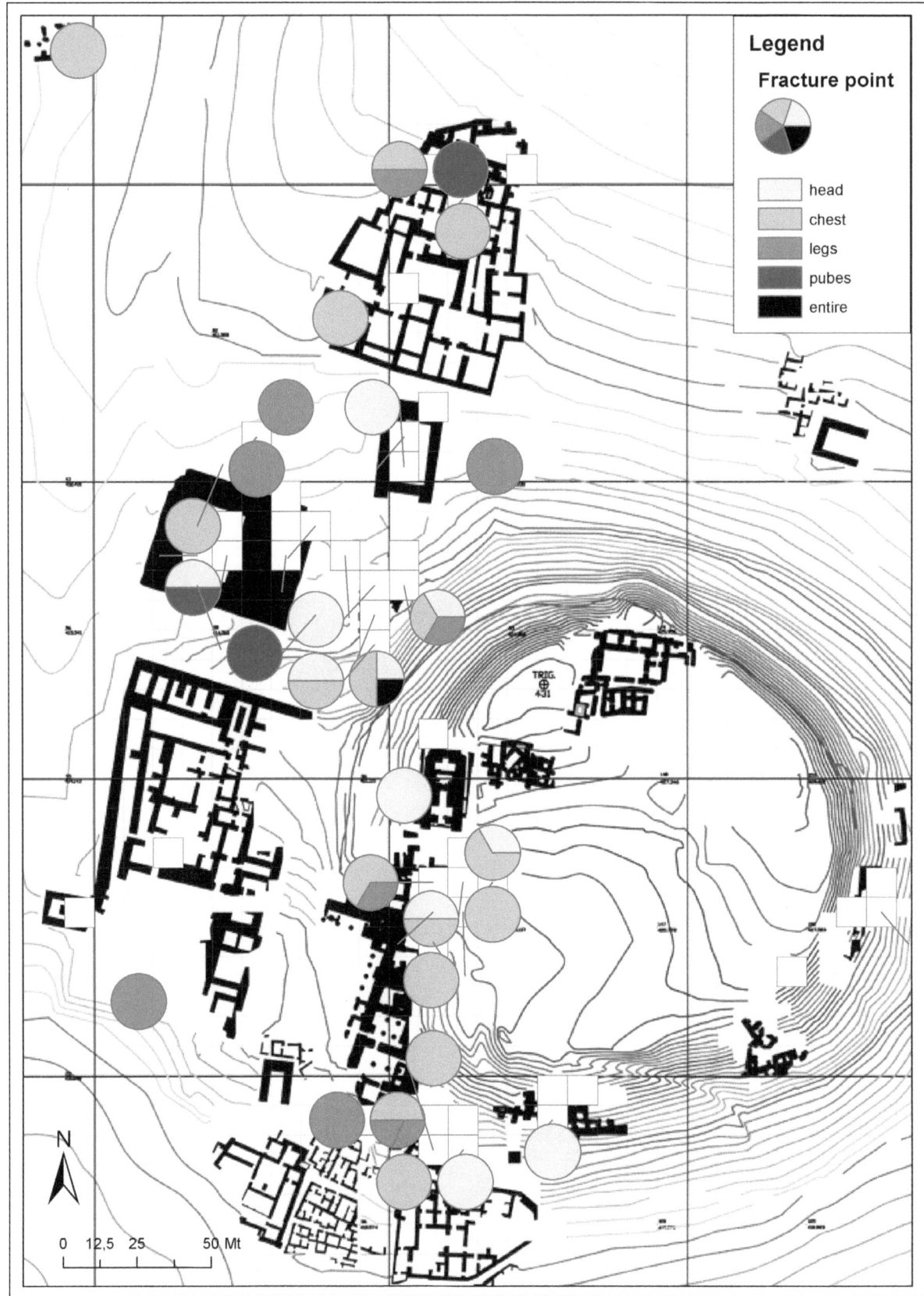

Table I:C. Spatial distribution of the 50 clay figurines Early Syrian breakages. © La Sapienza University of Rome ARCHEOSEMA Digital Archive.

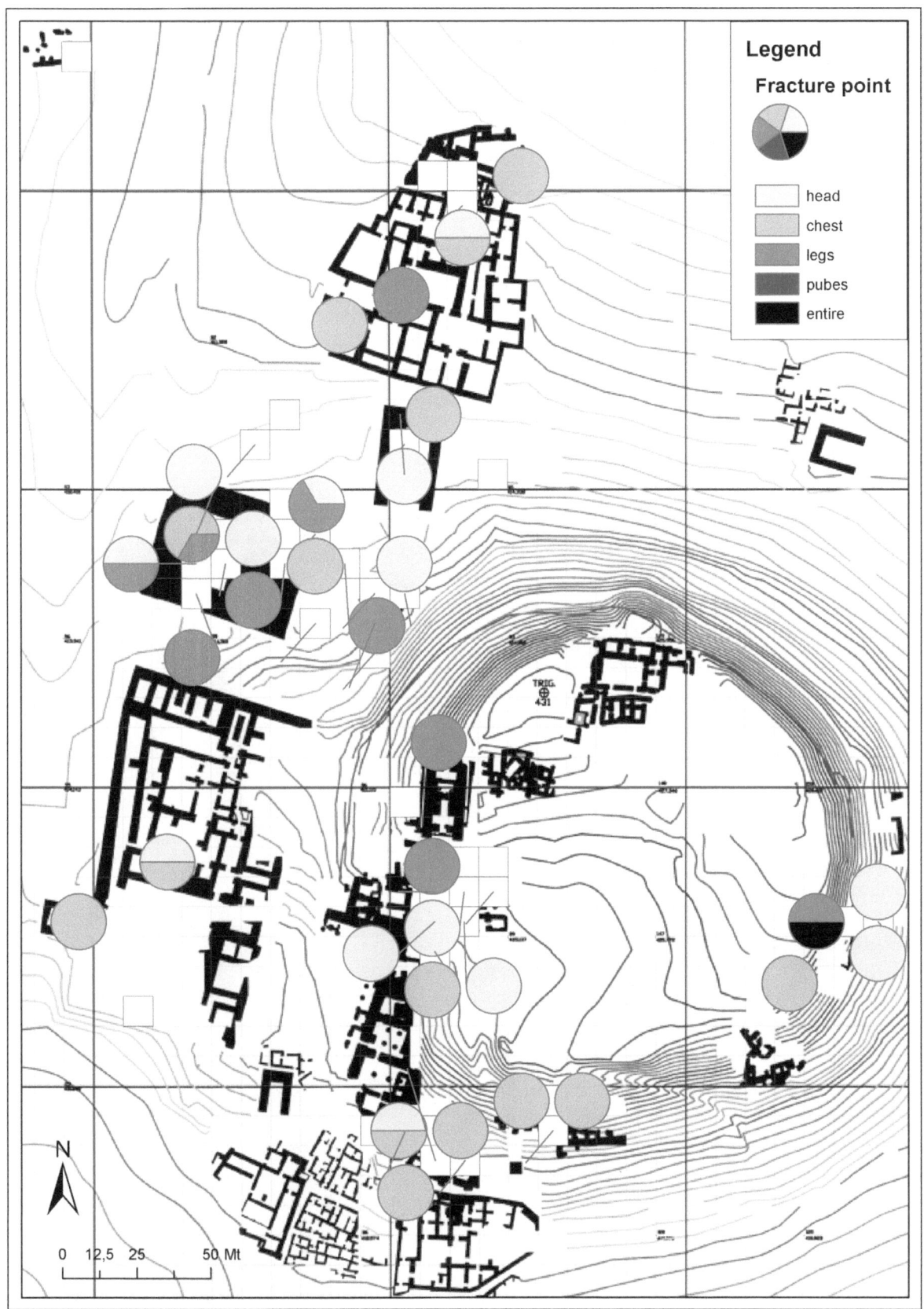

Legend

Fracture point

- head
- chest
- legs
- pubes
- entire

Table I:D. Spatial distribution of the 50 clay figurines, Old Syrian breakages. © La Sapienza University of Rome ARCHEOSEMA Digital Archive.

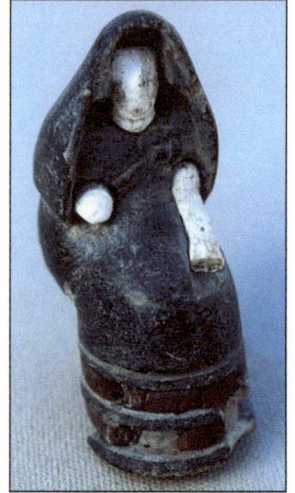
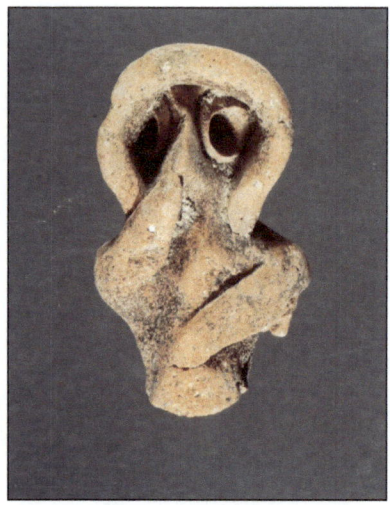

A. Clay Mimesis of archaic religious images (TM83G400 and TM94P666). (© La Sapienza University of Rome, Missione Archeologica Italiana in Siria)

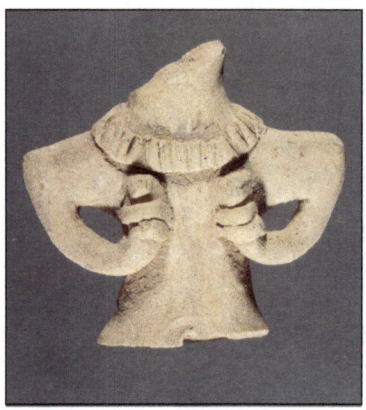
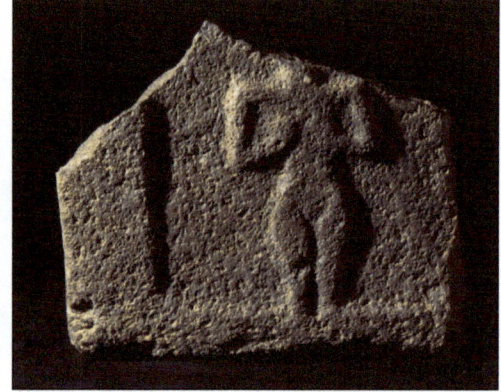

B) Clay Mimesis of the most popular sacred images (TM88R035 and TM08P2-916). (© La Sapienza University of Rome, Missione Archeologica Italiana in Siria)

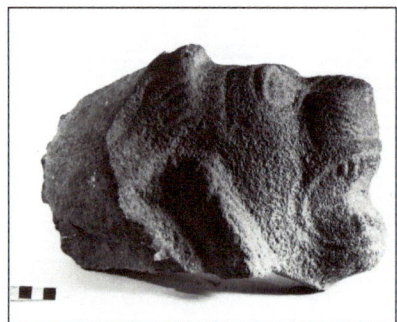

TM64B35

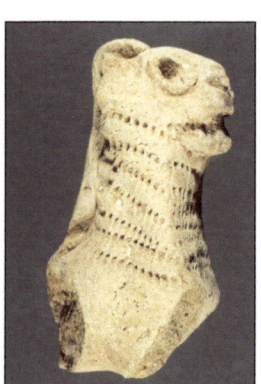

TM95P260

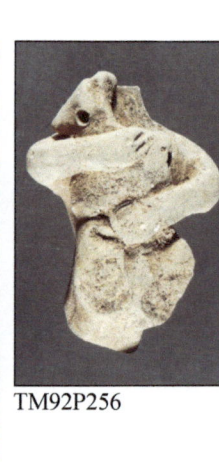

TM92P256

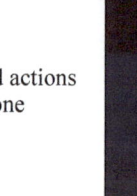

TM93P340

C) Clay Mimesis of the kingship symbols (TM64B35 and TM95P260) and actions (TM93P340 and TM92P256). (© La Sapienza University of Rome, Missione Archeologica Italiana in Siria)

Table II

came a professional medium to display a "potential automation" of the real world.[19] Thus we could hypothesize that the role of these infinite reproductions was that of collective copies created for some function during important rites, or to remain as memory signs, games, and/or allusions in daily life.[20]

THE CHEMICAL AND PHYSICAL ANALYSIS OF THE EBLA CLAY FIGURINES

Preliminary spectroscopic analysis realized in collaboration with CiSTEC at La Sapienza University of Rome by Professor Maria Laura Santarelli gave us the opportunity to analyze the technical aspects of the Early Syrian and Old clay figurine breakages and their topographic localizations, but the present analysis reveals a new side to the political assessment of the city, where the figurines became "clay images of people."[32] Our preliminary report on these Ebla figurines, which were richly embellished, has focused on the Sumerian concepts of clay as "creation matter" and as "molding technology."[33]

THE CHAÎNE OPÉRATOIRE OF THE EARLY SYRIAN AND OLD SYRIAN COROPLASTIC PRODUCTION

In the Sumerian tradition of the poem *Enki and Ninmakh*, Nammu, the mother of every god, pulls out the clay from the Apsû (The Primeval Ocean)[34] in order to put it in the matrix of the first man. This matrix, which was created by Enki *Nu.dím.mud*,[35] the artificer, will be used to make man a replicable "Automa" assigned to serve the gods, to obtain food for them, and to placate their wrath.[36] In this myth, the animation of the Automa through the life–giving breath of Ninmakh seems to create a solution for Enki's laziness.[37] This laziness is apparently incompatible with his well-known official status as Enki 'the wise," but perhaps here it is evident that in myth-genesis every contradiction should be resolved. Wisdom and guile are universal values of the intellect, but they are also able to invent human slavery.[38] Later, in the *Curse of Akkad*,[39] one of the most potent invectives against those whose commit sacrilege to injure the Ekur of Nippur (the House Temple of Enlil founded at the beginning of creation) is: "May your clay return to its Apsû; may it be clay cursed by Enki!" Afterwards, in the *Atramhasis*,[40] the Akkadian poem dated to the Hammurabi period, the birth–giver *belet–ili* is given instructions by Ea to mix the flesh and blood of a god with clay to produce mankind; and so the clay itself will be kneaded with the flesh and the blood of a sacrificed god, as if to emphasize a sort of "sacrifice

for life." Finally, the element of the Apsû–clay is eliminated altogether in the *Enuma Elish*,[41] when mankind will be created with only the blood of Kingu's corpse, the sacrificed rebel god. In this epic it seems that the clay matter of creation has been transfigured into an amalgam of the vital essence of humanity, adopting a function and a role that is easily understandable if analyzed from the point of view of original sin as the foundation of human life and as the separation between god and humans. In this Babylonian world clay always appears as the material and the ideal of every creation process. It is—in other words—a unique coexistence of values, ethics, and technologies that comprise allusive and metaphorical images, historical and meta-historical subjects. Clay is indeed a plastic material. However, both in the Sumerian and Akkadian texts, clay is not linguistically distinguished from mud. Modeling clay was used for the first Neolithic molded skull: the skull was removed from the face of the dead and was replaced by a plaster mask that reproduced the lines and attributes of the face, modifying and embellishing some details (Jericho, Palestine).[42] The sun–dried clay statues of Ain Ghazal in Jordan are exceptional coroplastic discoveries, which are already statuary, a coroplastic object that does not have miniature proportions, but nevertheless was discovered in contexts where there were miniature, handmade human and animal figurines.[43] The clay mask that transfigures the face of the dead and the clay reproductions of the family are archetypes, which, with plastic manipulation, gave the dead features from life, therefore the passage between the two—the *mask* and the *copy*[44]—were two of the most important nodes in the later consecration rites of divine statues.[45] In any case, the link between these theoretical, literary, and aesthetic notions can be identified in the Samarra figurines from Niniveh and Choga Mami, in the so-called Neolithic pillar figurines from Tell Bouqras, in the Yarim Tepe II anthropomorphic vessels, and later on in the snake-headed figurines of southern Mesopotamia dated to the end of the Ubaid period from Uruk, Oueili, Uqair, Ubaid, Ur, and Eridu. This is a homogeneous group of 20 hybrid figurines discovered out of their original contexts, apart from the Ur and Eridu copies, which were found in burials. The long heads, the almond-shaped eyes, the large shoulders, and the long legs are formal indices of the transformation of natural, human proportions: these elements make the body a model for a metamorphic change that, in this case, has been associated with a primeval aspect of Ninghizzida, the snake lord of the earth and the netherworld.[46] The metamorphism of these subjects depends on controlled manipulation of some details that could have had ideographic values (the faces, the eyes, the shoulders, the legs and the arms). This kind of alteration will be preserved through millennia as a technique to make the metamorphic clay figurines a sort of prosthesis of ostensible reality.[47] The well-known, ideological link between Mesopotamia and northern Syria has recently been detailed on a cognitive level.[48] But this link also is well documented by some imported clay figurines of the Early Bronze age probably coming from the central Euphrates region and by the extraordinary iconographic analogy between the Ubaid Mesopotamian clay figurines with almond-shaped eyes and two Eblaite figurines respectively from the Royal Palace G (TM93P589) and from the Area P (TM92P290).[49]

THEORETICAL APPROACHES TO THE VISUAL AND TACTILE MEANING OF THE EBLA CLAY FIGURINES

The miniature, or the idea of reproducing every subject of the imagination on a miniature scale, seems to be an ahistorical characteristic of perception,[50] which in the Near Eastern visual cultures becomes a tactile experience.[51] In this specific sense the Ebla clay figurines represent an extraordinary corpus,[52] since they can be studied as a contextual urban system of artefacts closely related both chronologically and culturally to the Mesopotamian psychical and technological milieu.[53] In the ancient myths of the Near East, clay is the matter, the matrix, and, at the same time, the body of the shape, as we say, the figure and substance of nature. Clay provides the possibility of replicating the one in the many, the copy and its twins, the unique and the diverse. Nevertheless, when we pass from this metaphor that lives in mythopoietic thought[54] and organizes the daily life of ancient people[55] to consider the physical properties of the clay, our attention is captured by its plastic essence, and we see the infinite forms that every lump of earth can take. It is as if the earth clod gave the hands also the capability of creation, modeling, and replication.[56] Starting from the Samarra, Halaf, and Ubaid periods, the additional elements that were molded, painted, impressed, and incised into the clay surfaces are the essence of the figure. These function as ideograms adapted to a model that seems standardized. These applications, impressions, and incisions are so typical of the Sumerian image perception and cognition that observing one single part both of the miniature composite statues and clay figurines of the Uruk

period, it is possible to reconstruct the semantic unity of the subjects (*pars pro toto*): the wheel of a ceremonial wagon, the instrument of a musician, the representative standard, the sex of the man and the woman, the human or deity's headgear, and so on. The impact of the agricultural revolution on the times and modes of the mass production of the clay figurines should not be forgotten or neglected.[57] However, the "symbolic revolution" behind these images seems to be extended to such a large geographical area that it is inappropriate to suggest an historical and cultural epicenter for human clay reproduction as an aesthetic aptitude,[58] the aptitude to organize shapes by integrating and aggregating elements as intelligible signs. At the same time, the high variability of attributes and subjects represented renders questionable the hypothesis that most of the ancient clay figurines were related to the first administrative processes[59] or dedicated to the mother goddess, to the fecundity of nature, and inspired by the family nucleus, intended as a microcosm of the whole society.[60] If this were the case, why the high frequency of clay figurines in pre-urban, archeological contexts and in the semi-nomadic, nomadic, and other scattered modern ethnographic groups? Why also the clay imitation of games, furnishings, hybrids, omens, and, more generally, many subjects and objects that frequently fall outside the control of our classification categories? In these reproductions an inner geometry is continuously translated, but into different shapes; the clothes are diversified but not exclusive; the roles are alluded to but not the hierarchy; the sexual attributes are almost always emphasized, but not the sexuality.[61] Moreover, the use of agglutination and incision of signs on standard clay models was the most useful, technical, and cognitive way to record action and desire on more profound, consolidated images of authority and institutions and to transfer these consolidated images to a living communication system.[62] Starting from the clay *replica* of the human world, the silent or non-verbal miniature replica of physical and metaphysical beings, it also will be possible to distinguish a figurative world from a non-figurative world, to reduce the world to a manual scale, and to make the hands' action on the clay an extension of human effectiveness on the present, on the past, and on the future, avoiding any written "dramatic" distinction between peoples and authority. In fact, in the ancient Near East we can identify historically what we call *image*[63] in our western culture many centuries later, probably reaching back to the Old Akkadian period when the word *salmu* translated from the Sumerian term ALAM denotes indifferently the representations of gods, kings, and human beings, as well as demons.[64] Since we considered the concept of "clay as matter creation" a human cognitive code for the reproduction and imitation of the human world, our proposal has been to verify how and where reproduction as creation began the *mimesis* of the physical and metaphysical worlds, first in Mesopotamia and later in Syria. In fact, between *creation* and *mimesis* is located the space of a rapid aesthetic transformation of these cultures and their communication systems.

NOTES

[1] The ARCHEOSEMA project (Geographic Information Systems and Artificial Adaptive Systems for the analysis of Complex Phenomena) of La Sapienza University of Rome, Department of Antiquities (Ramazzotti 2012c, pp. 6–10) gave me the financial support and the epistemological occasion to participate at the San Francisco workshop "Figuring Out: The Figurines of The Ancient Near East" organized by Stephanie Langin-Hooper (Ramazzotti 2012c, pp. 6–10; Ramazzotti, forthcoming c). This interdisciplinary workshop provided me with the opportunity to present a preliminary synthesis on Early Syrian (Early Bronze) and Old Syrian (Middle Bronze) clay figurines from Ebla-Tell Mardikh (Northern Syria), bringing together different ideas, concepts and materials that I began to collect after the interdisciplinary congress *Argilla. Storie di Terra Cruda* organized by me and by Giovanni Greco in Rome (25–26 May 2007: Ramazzotti – Greco 2011). For these reasons, I would like to thank Paolo Matthiae, Director of the Ebla Archaeological Mission for giving me the precious opportunity of studying these mostly unedited objects coming from the Ebla archaeological excavations; Armando Montanari, geographer of La Sapienza University of Rome, for his continuous support; Maria Laura Santarelli, engineer of La Sapienza University of Rome and coordinator of CISTEC (Laboratory of La Sapienza for materials and buildings techniques) for the chemical-physical analysis of the Ebla mud and clay world and Luca Deravignone and Irene Viaggiu, members of 'Archeosema Archaeological Group' for the geographical formalization and the spatial analysis on the Ebla Coroplastic Corpus (ECC) and, of course, Stephanie Langin-Hooper for inviting me to participate at this stimulating scientific and interdisciplinary workshop.

[2] In terms of absolute chronology, according to the so-called conventional Middle Chronology, the conquest of the first Ebla at the end of Early Bronze IV and the high Early Syrian period took place around 2300 B.C., while at the end of Early Bronze IVB and the late Early Syrian period, the destruction of the second Ebla should date from the years around 2000 B.C. The destruction of the third Ebla resulted in a catastrophic end of the urban life of the settlement in the final years of Middle Bronze II at the end of the classic Old Syrian period (Matthiae 1995, pp. 13–135). This probably took place immediately before the fall of Babylon in 1595 B.C., which meant the end of the Old Babylonian period in Southern Mesopotamia (Matthiae 2009, pp. 165–205, p. 165, footnote 3).

[3] See Ramazzotti 2003, pp. 15–71; Ramazzotti 2009a, pp. 193–202.

[4] See Ramazzotti 2011c, pp. 16–19. The problem of the identification of imported images could partially be solved with the chemical–physical analysis of the figurine's clay to determine its provenience; in any case the local imitation of foreign figurative models was also part of Ebla's aesthetic culture, deeply related to the lexical and conceptual translation of Sumerian and Early Dynastic written and visual documents. Ramazzotti 2010b, pp. 309–326; Ramazzotti 2013, pp. 161–216.

[5] Therefore, the plastic mold of "matter creation" began to copy the observed reality that the producer, free from the constraints and suggestions of customers, imagined in the clay. From our contemporary point of view, so deeply immersed in virtual communication, in the landscape of what is potential in nature, and in a world still oriented by the mass media, this miniature world, a tactile link between reality and imagination, appears far away and pervaded by abstractions and incongruities. However its ideographic character, its metamorphic physical structure and its 'genetic' hybridism reveals a tactile (and to us anachronistic) continuity between the similar and diverse, life and death, present and past. Ramazzotti 2011d, pp. 9–20; Ramazzotti 2012b, pp. 346–375; Ramazzotti 2013, pp. 48-69.

[6] We can suppose for this production not only faster, and almost industrial, firing methods that reduced the quality of the products, but also the influence of a specific role probably related to some pervasive religious cults, such as the Ishtar cult was at Ebla and Hadad at Aleppo. See Matthiae 2003b, pp. 381–402.

[7] The Early Syrian clay figurine typology has been proposed for Hama J: 1–6 (Fugmann 1958; Badre 1980, pp. 180), for the Orontes area (Badre 1980, pp. 52–54), for Tell Afis (Scandone Matthiae 1998, pp. 385–414; Scandone Matthiae 2002, pp. 16–18), for Umm el Marra (Petty 2007) for Tell Halawa and Tell Chuera (Meyer 2008, pp. 349–363), for Selenkahiye (Liebowitz 1988), for Tell Mumbaka-Ekalte (Czichon and Werner 1998), for Tell es-Sweyhat (Holland

1976, pp. 36–60), for Habuba Kebira (Heinrich et al 1970, pp. 27–85). The Ebla clay figurines were only preliminarily analyzed by Marchetti 2001, pp. 27–32; 62–64; 85–87 and Peyronel 2008, pp. 787–806.

[8] For the hybrid clay figurines dated to the Halaf and Ubaid period see Breniquet 2001, pp. 45–55.

[9] For the naturalistic clay representation in miniature scale of the Uruk period from Warka see Ziegler 1962; Wrede 1990, pp. 215–301; Wrede 1991; Wrede 2003.

[10] On the political and economic character of the 'Second Urban Revolution' in northern Mesopotamia see Ramazzotti 2002, pp. 651–752; Ramazzotti 2003, pp. 15–71; Ramazzotti 2009a, pp. 193–202.

[11] For the relative chronology of the Old Syrian Period based on historical, cultural and material cultural data see Nigro 2002b, pp. 297–328; Matthiae 2006c, pp. 39–51; Marchetti 2007, pp. 247–253; Matthiae 2007, pp. 6–33; Pinnock 2007, pp. 457–472.

[12] Marchetti 2000a, pp. 839–867; Marchetti 2000b, pp. 117–132; Marchetti 2001; Marchetti 2003, pp. 390–420; Marchetti 2007, pp. 247–283; Marchetti 2009, pp. 279–296; Di Michele 2010, pp. 145–154.

[13] Moreover during the Old Syrian period the human figurines are fashioned on standard schemes underlining their measures, proportions and sometimes social roles. Matthiae 1965, pp. 81–103; Baffi 1979, pp. 9–18; Marchetti 2000a, pp. 839–867; Marchetti 2000b, pp. 17–132; Marchetti 2001; Marchetti 2007, pp. 247–283.

[14] Ramazzotti 2009b, pp. 54–65; Ramazzotti 2011b, pp. 341–375.

[15] Dolce 1999, pp. 293–304; Dolce 2001, pp. 11–28; Archi aned Biga 2003, pp. 1–44.

[16] Some figurines dated to the Early Bronze IVB period were discovered in Area T (Matthiae 1993) and in the so–called Phase I of the Archaic Palace (Matthiae 2006a); recently some painted animals and human clay figurines were found in the Area HH where the 'Temple of the Rock' is located (Matthiae 2006b, pp. 447–493; Ramazzotti 2009, pp. 12–15). For some chronological aspects related to the EBIVB–MB transition at Ebla see Dolce 2008, pp. 171–194; Matthiae 2008, pp. 5–32.

[17] Like the so-called "undressed goddess", the "nude goddess with hands on her breasts" or the "doves of the goddess" closely related to the popular, rather than official, Old Babylonian and Old Syrian religious tradition. Pinnock 2000, pp. 127–134.

[18] Matthiae 2001, pp. 272–281.

[19] The case of the Early Dynastic, Early Syrian and then Old Babylonian, Old Syrian, and Middle Elamite wagons is typical; they are mobile, multi–sensory miniatures with tactile, visual, and sometimes olfactory functions. Each mechanism is activated by humans and is built as a harmonic integration of single parts (wheels, hubs, bodies, ropes). The parts are decorated with specific attributes (incised, applied. and integrated), which exhibit the complexity of a unitary project, or of a copy or simulation. A project that was probably planned in order to emulate, to memorize. or to reproduce ceremonial processions, on a different scale and in a different space–time dimension, like the ceremony attested in the L. 2769 Archive at Ebla, where the couple of divine, formally-dressed statues of Kura and Barama were certainly borne on a chariot drawn by oxen during the royal ritual. Matthiae 2007, pp. 270–311.

[20] Like the 2nd millennium Ishtar rite of Mari, where the hierarchical positions of the precious statues of deities were probably fixed in order to be seen. Following an Early Dynastic tradition from the Early Syrian period, many cult objects were transported inside chapels (DAGx) according to Biga (Biga 2006, pp.19–39), or sacred niches, such as the Ishkara image that we recently supposed was originally located in the painted niche of Building FF2 (Ramazzotti and Di Ludovico 2011, pp. 66–80; 2012, pp. 287–302); otherwise, in the contemporary Mesopotamian tradition these images of gods were set "upon" a seat in a temple so their surfaces could reflect (more than absorb) the light to render the physical emanation of the Sumerian (ME-LAM2) and Akkadian (*melammu*) as a sort of 'aura' according to Winter 1994, pp. 123–132.

[21] Ramazzotti 2011c, pp. 16–19.

[22] For a detailed analysis of this turtle discovered at Ebla see Marchetti 2009, pp. 275–296.

[23] The interpretation of the ancient Near East clay figurines is strictly related to the very different 'anthropomorphic' methods used for their classification see Van Buren 1931; Ucko 1962, pp. 38–54; Ellis 1967, pp. 51–61; Klengel and

Brandt 1967, pp. 19–28; Barrelet 1968; Hrouda, Braun, Holzinger 1981, pp. 61–67; Green 1983, pp. 87–96; Pinch 1983, pp. 405–414; Reiner 1988; Gimbutas 1989; Wiggerman 1986; 1992; Sycket 1992b, pp. 183–196; Pinch 1993; Brentijes 1994, pp. 15–18; Klengel and Brandt 1995, pp. 114–118; Ucko 1996, pp. 300–304; Tringham and Conkey 1998; Braun and Holzinger 1999, pp. 149–172; Pruß 2000, pp. 51–63; Pruß and Novák 2000, pp. 84–195; Malul 2001, pp. 353–367; Assante 2002, pp. 1–29; Nigro 2002a, pp. 1–11; King and Underhill 2002, pp. 707–714; Reade 2002, pp. 174–164; Martinez and Séve 2003, pp. 48–59; Marchetti 2003, pp. 247–283; Nakamura 2004, pp. 11–25; Moorey 2005; Kuijt and Chesson 2005, pp. 152–174; Meyer 2008, pp. 349–363; Abusch 2008, pp. 373–385; Waraksa 2008; Marchetti 2009, pp. 279–296; Pinch 2009; Waraksa 2009; Paradiso and Colantoni 2010, pp. 323–330; Ramazzotti, Deravignone,Viaggiu, forthcoming; Ramazzotti, forthcoming a; Ramazzotti, forthcoming d; Ramazzotti 2013, pp. 31-69.

[24] See Meyer 2008, pp. 349–363.

[25] See Marchetti and Nigro 1997, pp. 1–44; Marchetti and Nigro 2000, pp. 245–287.

[26] Marchetti 2009, pp. 279–296.

[27] Many inductions of cult images and "many rituals of constitution and installation" were attested in Mesopotamia from the end of the third Millennium, and a special verb meaning 'to give birth' (sum. *tud*; akk. *waladu*) is used for the creation of statues, rather than the verb 'to make' (DIM$_2$). see Walker and Dick 1999, pp. 55–122; Winter 2000a, pp. 129–162.

[28] Ramazzotti 2008a, pp. 191–205; 2009c, pp. 12–15; 2010, pp. 581–597.

[29] Peyronel 2008, pp. 787–806.

[30] Matthiae 2006b, pp. 447–493.

[31] We can consider the documented existence of some institutional rituals as official occasions also to realize clay reproductions. Examples are the monkey sacrifice at Mari and the equids sacrifice at Umm al-Marra. On the particular importance of equids in Syria during the Early Bronze Age Period see Biga 2007, pp. 125–151; for the supposed equids ritual dated to the Early Bronze Age period see Schwartz 2006, pp. 603–641; Schwartz 2007, pp. 39–68.

[32] Common everywhere as '*Volksgeister*' media of an inner communication inspired and supplied by the people's "common sense," sometimes intimate without explicit ideological constraints of the authorities, other times the quite instinctive reproduction of the real world as mysterious requests or questions for the venerated deities. For the archaeological context and the interpretation of the unbaked clay figurines discovered in the Favissa P. 9301 of Temple HH2 related to the Middle Bronze Age see Lisella 2010, pp. 821–836.

[33] Two MSAE (Materiali e Studi di Archeologia Eblaita) volumes related to about 4,500 fragments of Old Syrian Period clay figurines discovered at Ebla from 1981 to 2001 (a corpus that follows Marchetti's publication on the clay figurines discovered at Ebla between 1964 and 1980) is in preparation by the author (Ramazzotti, forthcoming b).

[34] The Apsû is usually intended as the 'Primeval Ocean' (Green 1978, pp. 127–167; Sjöberg 1994, pp. 202; Horowitz 1998, pp. 335) sustaining the Earthly and Kingship order (Ramazzotti 2009b, pp. 54–59), although the etymology of the word is still uncertain (Lambert 1997, pp. 75–77)

[35] The clay of the Apsû is plastic since the primeval ocean waters give the earth plasticity and therefore different images and shapes can be molded. In this specific character of the Apsû we should understand the epithet *Nu.dím.mud* (image fashioner, god of shaping) and this attribute gave Enki the protection of artisans and craftsmen. See Jacobsen 1971, pp. 111; Cavigneaux and Krebernik 1998–2001, pp. 607.

[36] We cannot exclude a particular version of the myth centered on the spontaneous birth of man from the Earth; in a second moment Enlil "broke through the cast of the earth with his newly created pickaxe so that the first man developed below could 'sprout forth.'" Kramer 1974, p. 5.

[37] See Kramer 1970, pp. 103–110; Kramer and Maier 1989, pp. 3–10; Cooper 1989, pp. 87–89; Black and Green 1992, pp. 75–76; Farber-Flügge 1995, pp. 287–292; Hallo 1996, pp. 231–234; Espak 2006.

[38] The first attempt by Enki to create mankind produces a visibly defective humanity of imperfect creatures; but the God will assign them a specific destiny (ME) and these ME will be existential archetypes of the human being. See

Castellino 1959, pp. 25–32; Oberhuber 1963, pp. 3–16; Farber-Flügge 1973; Matthiae 1984, pp. 7–37.

[39] Cooper 1983.

[40] Lambert and Millard 1999; Wilcke 1999, pp. 63–112.

[41] Maul 2000, pp. 23–34.

[42] Strouhal 1973; Ferembach 1977, pp. 179–181; Bienert 1991, pp. 9–23; Ramazzotti 2003, pp. 444–448; Ramazzotti 2012b, pp. 346–375.

[43] Rollefson 1986, pp. 45–52.

[44] Statues were also the object of recurrent renewal rites, such as the annual replacement of the silver mask that covered the statue of Kura at Ebla during the Early Syrian period. See, pp. Archi 2005, pp. 81–100; Archi 2010, pp. 3–17.

[45] Ramazzotti 2010b, pp. 309–326.

[46] Breniquet 2001, pp. 45–55.

[47] "The driving emotion in the making of these images was fear of bodily harm and an effort to find protection through the representation of the relevant superhuman figure." Porada 1995a, p. 10.

[48] On the figurative and cognitive relationship between the Mesopotamian Ubaid snake-headed human figurine and Old Syrian clay figurines from Ebla see Ramazzotti 2011, pp. 345–376.

[49] On the ideological relationship between the kingships of Ur and Ebla see Ramazzotti 2012b, pp. 346–375.

[50] For the logic of perception see Damerow 1996; Damerow 1998, pp. 247–269.

[51] Bailey 2005; Bailey, Cocjrane,Zambelli 2010; Ramazzotti and Greco 2011.

[52] The catalogues of the ancient Near East clay figurines from Syria, Mesopotamia and Egypt: Heuzey 1882; Legrain 1930; van Buren 1930; Opificius 1961; Ziegler 1962; Ucko 1968; Klengel-Brandt 1978; Littauer and Crowel 1979; Badre 1980; Wrede 1990, pp. 215–301; Wrede 1991, pp. 151–177; Pruß 1996; Spycket 1992a; Auerbach 1994; D'Amore 1998, pp. 75–98; Marchetti 2001; Moorey 2005; Teeter 2010; Pinnock 2011.

[53] Matthiae 1965, pp. 81–103; Baffi 1979, pp. 9–18; Marchetti 2000a, pp. 839–867; Pinnock 2000, pp. 127–134; Matthiae 2001, pp. 272–281; Marchetti 2009, pp. 279–296; Lisella 2010, pp. 821–836; Paradiso and Colantoni 2010, pp. 323–330.

[54] On the literary, aesthetic, and cognitive concept of the "thought that creates myths" see Frankfort 1948; Frankfort 1950; Groenewegen-Frankfort 1951; Jacobsen 1971; Frankfort 1992a, pp. 3–21; Frankfort 1992b, pp. 47–69; Frankfort et al 1946; 1949; Matthiae 1984; Matthiae 2003a, pp. 3–14. On the religious, cosmological, and literary texts related to the "thought that creates myths" in ancient Mesopotamia see Kramer 1964, pp. 149–142; Kramer 1972; Jacobsen 1976; Lambert 1975, pp. 42–65; Bottéro and Kramer 1992; Foster 1993; Lambert 1995, pp. 1825–1835; Black et al 2004.

[55] The historical reconstruction of the so-called "thought of the people" from the ancient Near Eastern archaeological documents is, of course, both a political and technical problem. I am convinced that the clay figurines will constitute an important set of data on which to build a "common sense" interpretation of propaganda and reduce historical reconstruction exclusively linked to the rhetoric of the ancient kingships. Here the use of "people" as an ambitious and complex heuristic category is acknowledged by Samuel Noah Kramer's (Kramer 1964) and Peter Roger Stuart Moorey's (Moorey 2003) pioneer works that philologically and archaeologically explored the natural limits of the textual, material, and aesthetic data.

[56] In this ancient repetition of manual creation and in its organization, some art historians have seen "La Vie des formes." On the other hand, cultures have always been considered more material the more they are tied to the Earth, and the more they are able to touch and model the earth. Material, in any case, is an ambiguous word, difficult to understand outside its human historiography. Ramazzotti 2010a, pp. 50–87.

[57] Cauvin 1994, Cauvin 2000.

[58] For the specific character of this 'aesthetic aptitude' in the southeastern European Neolithic see Bailey 2005.

[59] In particular see Schmandt-Besserat 1992, 1996.

[60] In particular see Gimbutas 1982, 1989, 1991. For a different model and quite opposite views see Ucko 1968, where the cultic role of the mother-goddess has been strongly criticized.

[61] On a more specific "gender approach" to the Near East clay figurines see Assante 2006, pp. 183; Pruß 2002, pp. 537–545; McCaffrey 2002, pp. 379–391; Garcia-Ventura and López-Bertran 2010, pp. 739–749.

[62] On this specific cognitive character of the ancient Mesopotamian figurative system see Ramazzotti 2010b, pp. 309–326; Ramazzotti, forthcoming a.

[63] On the ancient visual communication systems in the Babylonian cultures see Jacobsen 1987, pp. 1–11; Cooper 1990, pp. 109–116; Michalowski 1990, pp. 53–69; Winter 1995, pp. 2569–2580; Postgate 1994, pp. 176–184; Frankfort 1992b, pp. 47–69; Porada 1995b, pp. 2695–2714; Amiet 1997, pp. 321–337; Walken-Dijk 1999, pp. 55–122; Winter 2002, pp. 3–28; Bahrani 2002, pp. 15–22; Winter 2003, pp. 403–421; Bahrani 2003; Ramazzotti 2005, pp. 511–565; Winter 2007, pp. 117–142; Matthiae 2007, pp. 270–311; Ramazzotti 2007, pp. 7–20; Bahrani 2008, pp. 155–170; Ramazzotti 2011a, pp. 19–37; Ramazzotti 2013, pp.161-216.

[64] This will be the only definition both for the statues and for the stelae (sum. NA-RÚ-A; akk. from Sumerian loan: narû). For the stelae concept in the Ebla documents see Archi 1998, pp. 5–24.

BIBLIOGRAPHY

First International Congress 1, 2000	Proceedings of the First International Congress on the Archaeology of the Ancient Near East, Rome (May 18–May 23, 1998) 1. Problems of Chronology and Technology during the Bronze Age. Memory of the Past and Transmission of Images in the Artistic and Architectural Traditions. Change and Crisis: Archaeological Realities and Interpretative Models. Excavation and Survey Activities in the Nineties, P. Matthiae et al (eds.), Roma: Università degli studi di Roma "La Sapienza," Dipartimento di scienze storiche, archeologiche e antropologiche dell'antichita.
6th International Congress 1	Proceedings of the 6th International Congress of the Archaeology of the Ancient Near East (5 May–10 May, 2009), "Sapienza," Università di Roma, Volume 1: Near Eastern Archaeology in the Past, Present and Future. Heritage and Identity. Ethnoarchaeological and Interdisciplinary Approach, Results and Perspectives. Visual Expression and Craft Production in the Definition of Social Relations and Status, P. Matthiae et al (eds.), Harrassowitz Verlag-Wiesbaden.
6th International Congress 2	Proceedings of the 6th International Congress of the Archaeology of the Ancient Near East, (5 May–10 May, 2009), "Sapienza," Università di Roma, Volume 2: Excavations, Surveys and Restorations. Reports on Recent Field Archaeology in the Near East, P. Matthiae et al (eds.), Harrassowitz Verlag-Wiesbaden.
7th International Congress 2	Proceedings of the 7th International Congress on the Archaeology of the Ancient Near East (April 12– April 16, 2010), British Museum and UCL, London, 2. Ancient & Modern Issues in Cultural Heritage. Colour & Light in Architecture, Art & Material Culture. Islamic Archaeology, Roger Matthews, John Curtis (eds.), Wiesbaden: Harrassowitz Verlag.
Archi 1998	Archi, A., The Stele (na–rú) in the Ebla Documents, in Written on Clay and Stone. Ancient Near Eastern Studies Presented to K. Szarzynska, J. Braun et al (eds), Warsaw: AGADE, pp. 15–24.
Archi 2005	Archi, A., "The Head of Kura–The Head of Adabal," Journal of Near Eastern Studies 64, pp. 81–100.
Archi 2010	Archi, A., "Hadda of Alab and His Temple in the Ebla Period, Iraq 73, pp. 3–17.
Archi and Biga 2003	Archi, A. and Biga, M. G., A Victory over Mari and the Fall of Ebla. Journal of Cuneiform Studies 55, pp. 1–44.
Abusch 2008	Abusch, T., "Witchcraft Literature in Mesopotamia," in The Babylonian World, G. Leick (ed.), New York–London: Routledge, pp. 375–385.
Amiet 1997	Amiet P., "Anthropomorphisme et aniconisme dans l'antiquité orientale," Revue Biblique 104, pp. 321–337.

MARCO RAMAZZOTTI

Assante 2002	Assante, J., "Style and Replication in 'Old Babylonian' Terracotta Plaques: Strategies for Entrapping the Power of Images," in *Ex Mesopotamia et Syria Lux. Festschrift für Manfred Dietrich*, O. Loretz et al (eds.), Alter Orient und Altes Testament 281, Münster, Geburstag, pp. 1–29.
Assante 2006	"Undressing the Nude: Problems in Analyzing Nudity in Ancient Art, with an Old Babylonian Case Study," in *Images and Gender: Contributions to the Hermeneutics of Reading*, S. Schroer (ed.), Ancient Art , OBO 220, Freiburg–Göttingen 2006, pp. 177–208.
Astour 1992	Astour, M. C., "The Date of the Destruction of Palace G at Ebla," in *New Horizons in the Study of Ancient Syria*, M. W. Chavalas, J. L. Hayes (eds.), Bibliotheca Mesopotamica 22, Undena Publications, Malibu, pp. 29–39.
Auerbach 1994	Auerbach, E., *Terra Cotta Plaques from the Diyala and Their Archaeological and Cultural Contexts* (Ph.D. dissertation, The University of Chicago), Chicago.
Badre 1980	Badre, L*., Les figurines anthropomorphes en terre cuite à l'Age du Bronze en Syrie*, Bibliothèque archéologique et historique 103, Paris: P. Geuthner.
Baffi 1979	Baffi, F., "Su una figurina a stampo di età paleobabilonese da Ebla," *Vicino Oriente* 2, pp. 9–18.
Bahrani 2002	Bahrani, Z., "Performativity and Image: Narrative, Representation, and Uruk Vase," in *Leaving No Stones Unturned: Essay on the Ancient Near East and Egypt in Honor of Donald, P. Hansen*, E. Ehrenberg (ed.), Winona Lake: Eisenbrauns, pp. 15–22 .
Bahrani 2003	*The Graven Image. Representation in Babylonia and Assyria*, Philadelphia: University of Pennsylvania Press.
Bahrani 2008	Bahrani, Z., "The Babylonian Visual Image," in *The Babylonian World*, G. Leick (ed.), New York-London: Routledge, pp. 155–170.
Bailey 2005	Bailey, D. W., *Prehistoric Figurines. Representation and Corporeality in the Neolithic*, London – New York: Routledge.
Bailey, Cochrane, and Zambelli 2010	Bailey, D. W., Cochrane, D., Zambelli, J., *UNEARTHED: A Comparative Study of Jōmon Dogū and Neolithic Figurines*, Los Angeles: Sainsbury Centre for Visual Arts.
Barrelet 1968	Barrelet, M. T., "Figurines et reliefs en terre cuite de la Mésopotamie antique I: Potiers, termes de métier, procédés de fabrication et production," Paris: P. Geuthner.
Bienert 1991	Bienert, H. D., "Skull Cult in Prehistoric Near East," *Journal of Prehistoric Religion* 5, pp. 9–23.
Biga 2006	Biga, M. G., "Operatori cultuali a Ebla," *Studi Epigrafici e Linguistici sul Vicino Oriente Antico* 23, pp. 19–39.
Biga 2008	Biga, M. G., "Buried Among the Living at Ebla? Funerary Practices and Rites in a XXIV Century B.C. Syrian Kingdom," *Scienze dell'Antichità* 14, pp. 249–276.
Black and Green 1992	Black, J., Green, A., *Gods, Demons and Symbols of Ancient Mesopotamia: An Illustrated Dictionary*, London: University of Texas Press.
Black et al 2004	Black, J., et al, *The Literature of Ancient Sumer*, Oxford: Oxford University Press.
Bottéro and Kramer 1992	Bottéro, J., Kramer, S. N, *Uomini e dei della Mesopotamia*, Torino: Einaudi.
Braun-Holzinger 1999	Braun-Holzinger, E. A. , "Apotropaic Figures at Mesopotamian Temples in the Third and Second Millennia," in *Mesopotamian Magic: Textual, Historical, and Interpretive Perspectives*, T. Abusch, K. van der Toorn (eds.), Groningen: Brill, pp. 149–172.
Breniquet 2001	Breniquet, C., "Figurines Ophidienne," in *Ètudes Mésopotamiennes. Recueils de textes offert à Jean–Louis Huot*, C. Breniquet, C. Kepinski (eds.), Paris: Etudes et Recherche sur les Civilisations, pp. 45–55.
Brentjes 1994	Brentjes, B., "Terrakotta und Großplastik in Altvorderasien," in *Beschreiben und Deuten in der Archäologie des Alten Orients: Festschrift für Ruth Mayer-Opificius*, N. Cholidis (ed.), Altertumskunde des Vorderen Orients 4, Münster: Ugarit–Verlag, pp. 15–18.

Castellino 1959	Castellino, G. R., "Il concetto sumerico di "ME" nella sua accezione concreta," *Analecta Biblica* 12, pp. 25–32.
Cauvin 1994	Cauvin, J., *Naissance des divinités Naissance de l'agriculture. La Révolution des symboles au Néolithiques*, Paris: Flammarion.
Cauvin 2000	Cauvin, J., *The Birth of the Gods and the Origins of Agriculture*, Cambridge: Cambridge University Press.
Cavigneaux and Krebernik 1998–2001	Cavigneaux, A., Krebernik, M., "Nudimmud, Nadimmud," in *Reallexikon der Assyriologie* 9, p. 607.
Cooper 1983	Cooper, J., *The Curse of Agade,* Baltimore–London: John Hopkins University Press.
Cooper 1989	Cooper, J. "Enki's Member: Eros and Irrigation in Sumerian Literature," in *DUMU-EÛ-DUB-BA-A. Studies in Honor of Åke W. Sjöberg*, B. Hermann et al (eds.), Occasional Publications of the Samuel Noah Kramer Fund 11, Philadelphia: University Museum, p. 87–89.
Cooper 1990	Cooper, J., "Mesopotamian Historical Consciousness and the Production of Monumental Art in the Third Millennium B.C." in *Investigating Artistic Environments in the Ancient Near East,* A. C. Gunter et al (eds.), Washington: Arthur M. Sackler Gallery, Smithsonian Institution, pp. 109–116.
Czichon and Werner 1998	Czichon, R. M., Werner, P., *Tall Munbaqa-Ekalte* I. *Die bronzezeitlichen Kleinfunde. Ausgrabungen in Tall Munbáqa-Ekalte*, (Wissenschaftliche Veröffentlichungen der Deutschen Orient–Gesellschaft 97), Saarbrücken.
Damerow 1996	Damerow, P., *Abstraction and Representation: Essays on the Cultural Evolution of Thinking,* Dordrecht–Boston–London: Boston Studies in the Philosophy of Science.
Damerow, P., 1998	Damerow, P., "Prehistory and Cognitive Development," in *Piaget, Evolution, and Development*, J. Langer, M. Killen (eds.), Mahwah, New Jersey: Erlbaum, pp. 247–269.
Di Michele 2010	Di Michele, A., "Osservazioni sulla coroplastica antropomorfa del Bronzo Medio dall'area N di Tell Afis (Siria)," *Ocnus* 18, pp. 145–154.
Dolce 1999	Dolce, E., "The 'Second Ebla'. A View on the EB IVB City," *ISIMU: Revista sobre Oriente Próximo y Egipto en la antigüedad* 2, pp. 293–304.
Dolce 2001	Dolce, E., "Ebla after the 'Fall'— Some Preliminary Considerations on the EB IVB City," *Festschrift für Ali Abu Assaf, Damaszener Mitteilungen* 13, pp. 11–28.
Dolce 2008	Dolce, E., "Du Bronze Ancien IVB au Bronze Moyen à Ebla. Limites et problèmes pour une définition chronologique relative pendant la période de la ville protosyrienne récente," in *Proceedings 2008,* pp.15–29.
D'Amore 1998	D'Amore, P., "La coroplastica di Tell Afis," in *Tell Afis e l'Età del Ferro*, S. Mazzoni (ed.) Seminari di Orientalistica 2, Pisa 1998, pp. 75–98.
Ellis 1967	Ellis, R. S., "'Papsukkal' figures beneath the daises of Mesopotamian Temples," *Revue d'Assyriologie* 61, pp. 51–61.
Espak 2006	Espak, P., *Ancient Near Eastern Gods Enki and Ea: Diachronical Analysis of Texts and Images from the Earliest Sources to the Neosumerian Period,* Phd Dissertation, Tartu.
Farber-Flügge 1973	Farber-Flügge, G., *Der Mythos "Inanna und Enki" unter besonderer Berücksichtigung der Liste der me,* Studia Pohl. 10, Roma.
Farber-Flügge 1995	Farber-Flügge, G., ""Inanna and Enki' in Geneva: A Sumerian Myth Revisited," *Journal of Near Eastern Studies* 54, pp. 287–292.
Ferembach 1977	Ferembach, D., "Étude anthropologique. Les crânes surmodelés," in *Mémoire et Travaux du Centre de Recherches Préhistoriques Française de Jerusalem*, M. Lechevallier (ed.), Paris 1977, pp. 179–181.
Foster 1993	Foster, B., *Before The Muses: An Anthology Of Akkadian Literature.* Bethesda: University Press of Maryland.

Frankfort 1948	Frankfort, H., *Kingship and the Gods. A Study of Ancient Near Eastern Religion as the Integration of Society and Nature*, Chicago: Oriental Institute Essays.
Frankfort 1968	Frankfort, H., *The Birth of Civilization in the Near East,* New York: Garden City, N.Y.: Doubleday Anchor Books.
Frankfort 1992a	Frankfort, H., "Il dio che muore," in *Il dio che muore: mito e cultura nel mondo preclassico*, P. Matthiae (ed.), Firenze: La Nuova Italia, pp. 3–21.
Frankfort 1992b	Frankfort, H., "Il concetto di archetipo nella psicologia analitica e nella storia delle religioni," in *Il dio che muore: mito e cultura nel mondo preclassico*, Firenze: La Nuova Italia, pp. 47–69.
Fugmann 1958	Fugmann, E., *Hama. Fouilles et recherches de la Fondation Carlsberg 1931–1938. L'architecture des périodes pré-hellénistiques*, Copenhaghen.
Garcia-Ventura and López-Bertran 2010	Garcia-Ventura, A. López-Bertran, M., "Emboding Some Tell Asmar Figurines," in *6th International Congress* 1, pp. 739–749.
Gimbutas 1982	Gimbutas, M., *The Goddesses and Gods of Old Europe 6500–3500 B.C.: Myths and Cult Images*, Berkley: Thames & Hudson.
Gimbutas 1989	Gimbutas, M., *The Language of the Goddess,* San Francisco: Harper.
Gimbutas 1991	Gimbutas, M., *The Civilization of the Goddess*, San Francisco: Harper.
Groenewegen-Frankfort 1951	Groenewegen-Frankfort, H., *An Essay on Space and Time in the Representational Art of the Ancient Near East,* London: Harvard University Press.
Green 1983	Green, A., "Neo-Assyrian Apotropaic Figures: Figurines, Rituals and Monumental Art, with Special Reference to the Figurines from the Excavations of the British School of Archaeology in Iraq at Nimrud," *Iraq* 45, pp. 87–96.
Green 1978	Green, M. W., "The Eridu Lament," *Journal of Cuneiform Studies* 30, pp. 127–167.
Hallo 1996	Hallo, W. W., "Enki and the Theology of Eridu (review of Kramer, S. N., Maier, J., *Myths of Enki, The Crafty God*)," Journal of American Oriental Society 116, pp. 231–234.
Heinrich et al 1970	Heinrich, E. et al, "Zweiter vorläufiger Bericht über die von der Deutschen Orient–Gesellschaft mit Mitteln der Stiftung Volkswagenwerk in Habuba Kabira und in Mumbaqat unternommenen archäologischen Untersuchungen (Herbstkampagne 1969), erstattet von Mitgliedern der Mission," (Beilage 1–11), *Mitteilungen der Deutschen Orient Gesellschaft* 102, pp. 36–60.
Heuzey 1923	Heuzey, L., *Catalogue des figurines antiques de terre cuite. Figurines orientales et figurines des îles asiatiques (Musée national du Louvre)*, Paris: Musée nationaux.
Holland 1976	Holland, T. A., "Preliminary Report on the Excavations at Tell es-Sweyhat, Syria 1973–1974," *Levant* 8, pp. 36–60.
Horowitz 1998	Horowitz, W., *Mesopotamian Cosmic Geography*, Mesopotamian Civilization 8, Winona Lake: Eisenbrauns.
Hrouda and Braun-Holzinger 1981	Hrouda, B., Braun-Holzinger, E. A., "Figuren, Rundplastisch aus verschiedenem Material," in *"Figuren im Flachbild aus Ton" in Išin-Išan-Bahriyat* II, B. Hrouda (ed.), Münich 1981, pp. 61–67.
Jacobsen 1971	Jacobsen, Th., *Towards the Image of Tammuz and other Essays on Mesopotamian History and Culture*, Cambridge, MA: Cambridge University Press.
Jacobsen 1976	Jacobsen, Th.,*The Treasures of Darkness: A History of Mesopotamian Religion*, New Haven: Yale University Press.
Jacobsen 1987	Jacobsen, Th., "Pictures and Pictorial Language (the Burney Relief)," in *Figurative Language in the Ancient Near East*, M. Mindlin et al (eds.), London: Routledge, pp. 1–11.
King and Underhill 2002	King, R., Underhill, P. A., "Congruent Distribution of Neolithic Painted Pottery and Ceramic Figurines with Y-Chromosome Lineages," *Antiquity* 76, pp. 707–704.

Klengel-Brandt 1967	Klengel-Brandt, E., "Menschenfigurige Terrakotten aus Assur," *Forschungen und Berichte* 8, pp. 19–28.
Klengel-Brandt 1978	Klengel-Brandt, E., *Die Terrakotten aus Assur im Vorderasiatischen Museum Berlin*, Berlin.
Klengel-Brandt 1995	Klengel-Brandt, E., "Assyrian Terracotta Figurines," in *Discoveries at Ashur on the Tigris: Assyrian Origins,* P.O. Harper et al (eds.), New York, pp. 114–118.
Kuijt and Chesson 2004	Kuijt, M., Chesson, M. S, "Lumps of Clay and Pieces of Stone: Ambiguity, Bodies, and Identity as Portrayed in Neolithic Figurines," in *Archaeologies of the Middle East*, S. Pollock, R. Bernbeck (eds.), Oxford: John Wiley & Sons, pp. 152–174.
Kramer 1964	Kramer, S. N., "'Vox Populi' and the Sumerian Literary Documents," *Revue d'Assyriologie et d'Archéologie Orientale* 58, pp. 149–15.
Kramer 1970	Kramer, S. N., "Enki and His Inferiority Complex," *Orientalia* N.S. 39, pp. 103–110.
Kramer 1972	Kramer, S. N., *Sumerian Mythology: A Study of Spiritual and Literary Achievement in the Third Millennium B.C.* Philadelphia: University of Pennsylvania Press.
Kramer 1974	Kramer, S. N., "Thorkild Jacobsen: Philologist, Archaeologist, Historian, in *Sumerological Studies in Honor of Thorkild Jacobsen on His Seventieth Birthday,* S. J. Lieberman (ed.), Assyriological Studies 20, Chicago-London: Chicago: The Oriental Institute, pp. 1–8.
Kramer and Maier 1989	Kramer, S. N., Maier, J., *Myths of Enki, The Crafty God*, New York–Oxford: Oxford University Press.
Lambert 1975	Lambert, G. W., "The Cosmology of Sumer and Babylon," *Ancient Cosmologies*, C. Blacker, M. Loewe (eds.), London: Allen and Unwin, pp. 42–65.
Lambert 1995	Lambert, G. W., "Myth and Myth Making in Sumer and Akkad," in *Civilizations of the Ancient Near East* III, J. M. Sasson (ed.), New York: Hendrickson Publishers, pp. 1825–1835
Lambert 1997	Lambert, G. W., "The Apsû," *Rencontre Assyriologique Internationale* 44, 1997, pp. 75–77.
Lambert and Millard 1999	Lambert, G. W., Millard, A. R., *Atram-khasis. The Babylonian Story of the Flood*, Oxford: Eisenbrauns.
Legrain 1930	Legrain, L., *Terra-cottas from Nippur.* University of Pennsylvania, The University Museum. Publications of the Babylonian Section 16, Philadelphia.
Liebowitz 1988	Liebowitz, H., *The Oriental Institute Excavations at Selenkahiye, Syria. Terra-Cotta Figurines and Model Vehicles*, Bibliotheca Mesopotamica 22, Malibu: Crescent Academic Services.
Lisella 2010	Lisella, A. R., "The MBII Unbaked Clay Figurines from the Favissa P.9301 + P. 9308 in the Sacred area HH at Ebla," in *6th International Congress* 2, pp. 821–836.
Littauer and Crouwel 1979	Littauer, M. A., Crouwel, J. H., *Wheeled Vehicles and Ridden Animals in the Ancient Near East*, Handbuch der Orientalistik 1, Leiden: Brill Archive.
Malul 2001	Malul, M., "Foot Symbolism in the Ancient Near East: Imprinting Foundlings' Feet in Clay in Ancient Mesopotamia," *Zeitschrift für altorientalische und biblische Rechtsgeschichte* 7, pp. 353–367.
Marchetti 2000a	Marchetti, N., "Clay Figurines of the Middle Bronze Age from Northern Inner Syria: Chronology, Symbolic Meaning and Historical Relations," in *First International Congress,* pp. 839–867.
Marchetti 2000b	Marchetti, N., "A Middle Bronze I Ritual Deposit from the Amuq Plain: Note on the Dating and Significance of the Metal Anthropomorphic Figurines from Tell Judaidah," *Vicino Oriente* 12, pp. 117–132.
Marchetti 2001	Marchetti, N., *La coroplastica eblaita e siriana nel Bronzo Medio. Campagne 1964–1980*, Materiali e Studi Archeologici di Ebla V, Rome: Sapienza University Press.
Marchetti 2003	Marchetti, N., "Workshops, Trading Routes and Divine Figures. On the Early Middle Bronze II Syro-Anatolian Lead Figurines," *Orientalia* NS 72/4, pp. 390–420.
Marchetti 2007	Marchetti, N., "Chronology and Stratification of Middle Bronze Age Clay Figurines in Syria and Northern Palestine," in *Proceedings* 2007, pp. 247–283.

Marchetti 2009	Marchetti, N., "Divination at Ebla during the Old Syrian Period: The Archaeological Evidence," *Essays in Honor of Lawrence E. Stager*, J. D. Schloen (ed.), Winona Lake: Eisenbrauns, pp. 279–296.
Marchetti and Nigro 1996	Marchetti, N., Nigro, L., "Cultic Activities in the Sacred Area of Ishtar at Ebla During the Old Syrian Period: The Favissae F. 5327 and F. 5238," *Journal of Cuneiform Studies* 49, pp. 1–44.
Marchetti and Nigro 2000	Marchetti, N., Nigro, L., "The Favissa F. 5238 in the Sacred Area of Ishtar and the Transition from the Middle Bronze I to the Middle Bronze II at Ebla," *Languages and Cultures in Contact. At the Crossroads of Civilizations in the Syro–Mesopotamian Realm*, K. Van Lerberghe, G. Voet (eds.), Orientalia Lovaniensia Analecta 96, pp. 245–287.
Martinez-Sève 2003	Martinez-Sève, L., Sur les figurines animalières de Suse (Iran), *Anthropozoologica* 38, pp. 49–59.
Matthiae 1965	Matthiae, P., "Le figurine in terracotta," in *Missione Archeologica Italiana in Siria. Rapporto preliminare della campagna 1964*, P. Matthiae (ed.), Roma: Università di Roma La Sapienza, pp. 81–103.
Matthiae 1984	Matthiae, P., *Il sovrano e l'opera. Arte e potere nella Mesopotamia antica*. Roma – Bari: Laterza.
Matthiae 1989	Matthiae, P., "Destruction of Ebla Royal Palace: Interconnections between Syria, Mesopotamia and Egypt in the Late EB IVA," *High, Middle, or Low? Acts of an International Colloquium on Absolute Chronology held at the University of Gothenburg, 20th–22nd August 1987*, P. Åström, Gothenburg: P. Åströms förlag, pp. 163–169.
Matthiae 1993	Matthiae, P., "L'aire sacreée d'Ishtar à Ebla: Résultats des fouilles de 1990–1992," *Comptes rendus de l'Académie des inscriptions et belles–lettres* 1993, pp. 613–662.
Matthiae 2001	Matthiae, P., "The Face of Ishtar of Ebla," in *Beiträge zur Vorderasiatische Archäologie, Winfried Orthmann gewidmet*, J-W. Meyer et al (eds.), Frankfurt am Main, pp. 272–281, pp. 272–281.
Matthiae 2003a	Matthiae, P., "History of Art in the Ancient Near Eastern Archaeology: Problems and Perspectives," *Contributi e Materiali di Archeologia Orientale* 9, pp. 3–13.
Matthiae 2003b	Matthiae, P., "Ishtar of Ebla and Hadad of Aleppo: Notes on Terminology, Politics and Religion of Old Syrian Ebla," in *Semitic and Assyriological Studies Presented to P. Fronzaroli by Pupils and Colleagues*, P. Marrassini (ed.) Wiesbaden: Eisenbrauns, pp. 381–402.
Matthiae 2006a	Matthiae, P., "The Archaic Palace at Ebla: A Royal Building between Early Bronze Age IVB and Middle Bronze Age I," in *Confronting the Past. Archaeological and Historical Essays on Ancient Israel in Honor of William G. Dever*, S. Gitin et al (eds.), Winona Lake: Eisenbrauns, pp. 85–103.
Matthiae 2006b	Matthiae, P., "Un grande temple de l'époque des archives dans l'Ébla protosyrienne: fouilles à Tell Mardikh 2004–2005," *Comptes rendus de l'Académie des inscriptions et belles–lettres*, pp. 447–493.
Matthiae 2006c	Matthiae, P., "Archaeology of a Destruction: The End of MBII Ebla in the Light of Myth and History," in Timelines. Studies in Honour of Manfred Bietak, Orientalia Lovaniensia Analecta 149, E. Czerny et al (eds.), Leuven: Peeters, pp. 39–51.
Matthiae 2007	Matthiae, P., "The Standard of the Maliktum of Ebla in the Royal Archives Period," *Zeitschrift für Assyriologie* 99, pp. 270–311.
Matthiae 2008	Matthiae, P., "The Destruction of Old Syrian Ebla at the End of Middle Bronze II. New Historical Data," in *Proceedings* 2008, pp. 3–35.
Matthiae 2009	Matthiae, P., "Crisis and Collapse: Similarity and Diversity in the Three Destruction of Ebla from EBIVA to MBII," *Scienze dell'Antichità* 15, pp. 165–204.
Maul 2000	Maul, S., "Il ritorno alle origini: 'Il rinnovamento rituale' della regalità nella festa babilonese–assira del nuovo anno," *Il giubileo prima del giubileo. Tempo e spazio nelle civiltà mesopotamiche e dell'antico Egitto*, Aa. (eds.), Atti del Convegno Internazionale, Milano, pp. 23–34.

Maul 2007	Maul, S., "Divination Culture and Handling of the Future," in *The Babylonian World*, G. Leick (ed.), New York–London, pp. 361–372.
Mazzoni 1985	Mazzoni, S., "Elements of the Ceramic Culture of Early Syrian Ebla in Comparison with Syro-Palestinian EBIV," *Bulletin of the American School of Oriental Research* 257, pp. 3–8.
Mazzoni 2002	Mazzoni, S., "The Ancient Bronze Age Pottery Tradition in Northwestern Central Syria," in *Céramique de l'Age du Bronze en Syrie, I. La Syrie du Sud et la Vallée de l'Oronte*, M. al-Maqdissi et al (eds.), Bibliothèque Archèologique et Historique 161, Beyrouth, pp. 69–96.
McCaffrey 2002	McCaffrey, K., "Reconsidering Gender Ambiguity in Mesopotamia: Is a Beard Just a Beard?" in *Sex and Gender in the Ancient Near East*, A. Parpola, M.C. Whiting (eds.), Helsinki: University of Helsinki Press, p. 379–391.
Meyer 2008	Meyer, J-W., "The Anthropomorphic Terracotta Figurines from Tell Chuera and Halawa: Their Chronology and Their Meaning," in *Proceedings* 2008, pp. 349–363.
Michalowski 1990	Michalowski, P., "Early Mesopotamian Communicative Systems: Art, Literature and Writing," in *Investigating Artistic Environments in the Ancient Near East*, A. C. Gunter (ed.), Washington: University of Wisconsin Press, pp. 53–69.
Moorey 2003	Moorey, P. R. S., *Idols of the People. Miniature Images of Clay in the Ancient Near East*, Oxford: Oxford University Press.
Moorey 2005	Moorey, P. R. S., *Ancient Near Eastern Terracottas with a Catalogue of the Collection in the Ashmolean Museum*, Oxford: Ashmolean Museum.
Nakamura 2004	Nakamura, C., "Dedicating Magic: Neo–Assyrian Apotropaic Figurines and the Protection of Assur," *World Archaeology* 36, pp. 11–25.
Nigro 2002a	Nigro, L., "A Female Clay Figurine from Tell Agrab (Iraq) in the Vatican Museum," *Direzione dei Musei Stato della Città del Vaticano* 22, pp. 1–11.
Nigro 2002b	Nigro, L., "The MB Pottery Horizon of Tell Mardikh/Ancient Ebla in a Chronological Perspective," *The Middle Bronze Age in the Levant. Proceedings of an International Conference on MB IIA Ceramic Material*, Vienna, 24th–26th of January 2001, M. Bietak (ed.), Wien: Verlag der Österreichischen Akademie der Wissenschaften, pp. 297–328.
Oberhuber 1963	Oberhuber, K., "Der numinose Begriff ME im Sumerischen," *Innsbrucker Beiträge zur Kulturwissenschafte*, Sonderheft 17, pp. 3–16.
Opificius1961	Opificius, R., *Das altbabylonische Terrakottarelief*, Untersuchungen zur Assyriologie und vorderasiatischen Archäologie 2, Berlin 1961.
Paradiso and Colantoni 2010	Paradiso, S., Colantoni, A., "Clay Anthropomorphic Figurines of the Late Bronze Age from Northern Inner Syria: Typological Development of a Typical Craft Production," in *4th International Congress,* pp. 323–330.
Peyronel 2008	Peyronel, L., "Making Images of Humans and Animals. The Clay Figurines from the Royal Palace G at Tell Mardikh-Ebla, Syria (EB IVA, c. 2400–2300 BC)," in *Proceedings of the 5th International Congress on the Archaeology of the Ancient Near East,* Madrid 2006, J. Mª Córdoba et al (eds.), Madrid: Consejo Superior de Investigaciones Cientificas (CSIC), pp. 787–806.
Petty 2007	Petty, A., *Bronze Age Anthropomorphic Figurines from Umm el-Marra, Syria*, Oxford: British Archaeological Reports.
Pinch 1983	Pinch, G., "Childbirth and Female Figurines at Deir el-Medina and el-'Amarna," *Orientalia* 52, pp. 405–414.
Pinch 1993	Pinch, G., V*otive Offerings to Hathor*, Oxford: Griffith Institute/Clarendon Press.
Pinch 2009	Pinch, G., *Magic in Ancient Egypt*, Austin: University of Texas Press.

Pinnock 2000	Pinnock, F., "The Doves of the Goddess: Elements of Ishtar's Cult in Middle Bronze Ebla," *Levant* 32, pp. 127–134.
Pinnock 2007	Pinnock, F., "Middle Bronze Age Ceramic Horizon at Ebla. Typology and Chronology," *Proceedings* 2007, pp. 457–472.
Pinnock 2011	Pinnock, F., *Le giarette con decorazione applicata del Bronzo Medio* II, Materiali e Studi Archeologici di Ebla IX, Roma: Università degli studi di Roma "La Sapienza."
Porada 1995a	Porada, E., *Man and Images in the Ancient Near East*, London: Moyer Bell.
Porada 1995b	Porada, E., Understanding Ancient Near Eastern Art: a Personal Account, in *Civilizations of the Ancient Near East*, IV, J. M. Sasson (ed.), New York: Hendrickson, pp. 2695–2714.
Postgate 1994	Postgate, N, "Text and figure in Mesopotamia," in *The Ancient Mind. Elements of Cognitive Archaeology*, C. Renfrew, E. B. W. Zubrow (eds.), Cambridge, MA: Cambridge University Press, pp. 176–184.
Pruß 1996	Pruß, A., *Die Amuq-Terrakotten. Untersuchungen zu den Terrakotta-Figuren des 2. und 1. Jahrtausends v.Chr. aus den Grabungen des Oriental Institute Chicago in der Amuq-Ebene*, Halle-Wittenberg.
Pruß 2000	Pruß, A., "Patterns of Distribution: How Terracotta Figurines were Traded," *Transeuphratène* 19, pp. 51–63.
Pruß 2002	Pruß, A., "The Use of Nude Female Figurines," in *Sex and Gender in the Ancient Near East, Proceedings of the 47th Rencontre Assyriologique Internationale*, Helsinki 2001, S. Parpola, R. M. Whiting (eds.), Helsinki: Eisenbrauns, pp. 537–545.
Pruß and Novák 2000	Pruß, A., Novák, M, "Terrakotten und Beinidole in sepulkralen Kontexten," *Archiv für Orientsforschung* 27/1, pp. 84–195.
Ramazzotti 2002	Ramazzotti, M., "La 'Rivoluzione Urbana' nella Mesopotamia meridionale. Replica 'versus' processo. *Accademia Nazionale dei Lincei. Classe delle Scienze Morali Storiche e Filologiche, Rendiconti*, Serie 9,13, pp. 651–752.
Ramazzotti 2003a	Ramazzotti, M., "Modelli insediamentali alle soglie del Protodinastico in Mesopotamia meridionale, centrale e nord-orientale. Appunti per una critica alla formazione 'secondaria' degli stati nel III Millennio a.C.," *Contributi e Materiali di Archeologia Orientale* 9, pp. 15–71.
Ramazzotti 2003b	Ramazzotti, M., "Recensione al volume *Ramad. Site néolithique en damascène (Syrie) aux VIIIe et VIIe millénaires avant l'ère chrétienne*, *Orientalia* 72/4, pp. 444–448.
Ramazzotti 2005	Ramazzotti, M., "Segni, codici e linguaggi nell''agire comunicativo' delle culture protostoriche di Mesopotamia, alta Siria e Anatolia, in *Ina Kibrat Erbetti: Studies in Honor of Paolo Matthiae Offered by Colleagues and Friends on the Occasion of His 65th Birthday*, F. Baffi et al (eds.), Rome: Sapienza Università Editrice, pp. 511–565.
Ramazzotti 2007	Ramazzotti, M., "NU.GIRI12: il Giardiniere di Babilonia, *Automata. Journal of Nature, Science and Technologies in the Ancient World* 2, pp. 7–20.
Ramazzotti 2008	Ramazzotti, M., "An Integrated Analysis for the Urban Settlement Reconstruction. The Topographic, Mathematical and Geophysical Frame of Tell Mardikh, Ancient Ebla," in *4th International Congress*, pp. 191–205.
Ramazzotti 2009a	Ramazzotti, M., "Lineamenti di archeologia del paesaggio mesopotamico. Descrizioni statistiche e simulazioni artificiali adattive per un'analisi critica della demografia sumerica e accadica," in *Geografia del popolamento*, G. Macchi Jánica (ed.), Siena: Fieravecchia, pp. 193–202.
Ramazzotti 2009b	Ramazzotti, M., "A Presage of Heresy. Metaphysical Notes and Iconographic Themes for an Archaeology of the Mesopotamian Skies," in *Galileo. Images of the Universe from Antiquity to the Telescope*, P. Galluzzi (ed.), Firenze: Giunti, pp. 54–65.

Ramazzotti 2009c	Ramazzotti, M., "Dall'automazione del record geomagnetico alla scoperta del Tempio della Roccia (2400 – 2350 a. C. circa)," *Archeomatica* 0, pp. 12–15.
Ramazzotti 2010a	Ramazzotti, M., *Archeologia e semiotica. Linguaggi, codici, logiche e modelli*, Torino: Bollati Boringhieri.
Ramazzotti 2010b	Ramazzotti, M., "Ideografia ed estetica della statuaria mesopotamica del III millennio a. C., in *Ana turri gimilli. Studi dedicati al Padre Werner R. Mayer, S.J. da amici e allievi*, M. Liverani, M. G. Biga (eds.), Quaderni del Vicino Oriente V, Roma: Sapienza Università Editrice, pp. 309–326.
Ramazzotti 2010c	Ramazzotti, M., "The Ebla Archaeological Park. Natural, Archaeological and Artificial Italian Portrait of the Ancient Syrian Capital, in *6ᵗʰ International Congress*, 581–597.
Ramazzotti 2011a	Ramazzotti, M., "SIG4. Il mattone. Natura, tecniche e coscienze edili nell'antica Mesopotamia," *Automata. Journal of Nature, Science and Technologies in the Ancient World* 3–4, pp. 19–37.
Ramazzotti 2011b	Ramazzotti, M., "Anatomia di Akkad. Le ombre di una città invisibile dal suo paesaggio storiografico, estetico e storico," in *Quale Oriente? Omaggio a un Maestro. Studi di Arte e di Archeologia del Vicino Oriente in memoria di A. Moortgat a trenta anni dalla sua morte*, R. Dolce (ed.), Palermo: Flaccovio, pp. 341–375.
Ramazzotti 2011c	Ramazzotti, M., "Dalla 'materia della creazione' alle prime 'tecniche dell'automazione.' Un microscopio sulla coroplastica arcaica del Vicino Oriente," *Archeomatica* 2, pp. 16–19.
Ramazzotti 2011d	Ramazzotti, M., "Argilla. Mito, storia e archeologia della terra cruda nell'antica Mesopotamia," in *Argilla. Storie di terra cruda*, M. Ramazzotti, G. Greco (eds.), Roma: Artemide, pp. 9–20.
Ramazzotti 2012a	Ramazzotti, M., "The Ideological and Aesthetic Relationship Between Ur And Ebla During the Third Millennium B. C., in *7ᵗʰ International Congress*, pp. 53–72
Ramazzotti 2012b	Ramazzotti, M., "Aesthetic and Cognitive Report on Ancient Near Eastern Clay Figurines, Based on Some Early Bronze and Middle Bronze Records Discovered at Ebla-Tell Mardikh (Syria), *Scienze dell'Antichità* 17, pp. 346–375.
Ramazzotti 2012c	Ramazzotti, M., "ARCHEOSEMA. Un modello archeo-logico per la ricerca teorica, analitica e sperimentale del fenomeni complessi. *Archeomatica* 2, pp. 6–10.
Ramazzotti 2013	Ramazzotti, M., *Mesopotama antica. Archeologia del pensiero creatore di miti nel Paese di Sumer e di Accad*, Roma: Artemide.
Ramazzotti, forthcoming a	Ramazzotti, M., "The Aesthetical Lexicon of Ebla's Composite Art During the Age of the Archives. An Innovative Visual Representation of Words and Concepts Inside the Early Dynastic Technology of the Images, in Aa. (eds.) *Proceedings of the 8th International Congress on the Archaeology of the Ancient Near East, Rome 2012*.
Ramazzotti, forthcoming b	Ramazzotti, M., "Le figurine fittili di Ebla nelle fasi del BMI–II. Il 'corpus' documentario riferito alle annate di scavo 1981–2001," *Materiali e Studi di Archeologia Eblaita*, Roma: Sapienza Università Editrice.
Ramazzotti forthcoming c	Ramazzotti, M., "Archeosema. Geographic Information System and Artificial Adaptive Systems for the Complex Phenomaena Analysis," Archeologia e Calcolatori Special Issue in Honor of David L. Clarke, in *ARCHEOSEMA*, M. Ramazzotti (ed.), Firenze: All'Insegna del Giglio.
Ramazzotti and Di Ludovico 2011	Ramazzotti, M., Di Ludovico, A., "Design at Ebla. The Decorative System of a Painted Wall Decoration," *Orientalia* 80/1, pp. 66–80.
Ramazzotti and Di Ludovico 2012	Ramazzotti, M., Di Ludovico, A., "White, Red and Black. Technical Relationships and Stylistic Perceptions between Colours, Lights and Places in Mesopotamia and Syria during the Third Millennium BC." in *7th International Congress,* pp. 287–302.
Ramazzotti and Greco 2011	Ramazzotti, M. Greco, G.(eds.), *Argilla. Storie di terra cruda*, Roma: Artemide.

Ramazzotti, Deravignone, and Viaggiu, forthcoming	Ramazzotti, M., Deravignone, L., Viaggiu, I., "Taxonomy, Modelling & Neural Networks applied to the Ebla Coroplastic Corpus of the Early Syrian and Old Syrian Period," in *ARCHEOSEMA*, M. Ramazzotti (ed.), Roma: Sapienza Università Editrice.
Reade 2002	Reade, J., "Unfired Clay, Models, and 'Sculptor Models' in the British Museum," *Archiv für Orientforschung* 48–49, pp. 147–164.
Reiner 1988	Reiner, E., "Magic Figurines, Amulets and Talismans," in *Monsters and Demons in the Ancient and Medieval Worlds. Papers Presented in Honor of Edith Porada*, A. E. Farkas et al (eds.), Mainz on Rhine: Philipp von Zabern.
Proceedings 2007	*Proceedings of the International Colloquium From Relative Chronology to Absolute Chronology: The Second Millennium B.C. in Syria-Palestine*, P. Matthiae et al (eds.), Roma: Bardi Editore.
Proceedings 2008	*Proceedings of the International Colloquium From Relative Chronology to Absolute Chronology: The Second Millennium B.C. in Syria-Palestine*, P. Matthiae et al (eds.), Roma: Bardi Editore.
Rollefson, G. O. 1986	Rollefson, G. O., "Neolithic at 'Ain–Ghazal (Jordan): Ritual and Ceremony, II," *Paléorient* 12/1, pp. 45–52.
Schmandt-Besserat 1992	Schmandt-Besserat, D., *Before Writing. From Counting to Cuneiform*, Austin: University of Texas Press.
Schmandt-Besserat 1996	Schmandt-Besserat, D., *How Writing Come About*, Austin: University of Texas Press.
Scandone Matthiae 1998	Scandone Matthiae, G., "La coroplastica del Bronzo Antico IV e del Bronzo Medio II," in *Tell Afis (Siria). Scavi sull'Acropoli 1988–1992*, S. M. Cecchini, S. Mazzoni (eds.), Pisa: ETS, pp. 385–414.
Scandone Matthiae 2002	Scandone Matthiae, G., "Area B: la coroplastica del Bronzo Antico IVA–B e del Bronzo Medio II," in "Tell Afis (Siria) 2000–2001," S. Mazzoni et al (eds.), *Egitto e Vicino Oriente* 25, pp. 16–18.
Schwartz et al 2006	Schwartz, G. et al, "A Third–Millennium B.C. Elite Mortuary Complex at Umm el-Marra, Syria: 2002 and 2004 Excavations, *American Journal of Archaeology* 110, pp. 603–641.
Schwartz 2007	Schwartz, G., Status, "Ideology and Memory in Third–Millennium Syria: 'Royal' Tombs at Umm el-Marra," in *Performing Death. Social Analyses of Funerary Traditions in the Ancient Near East and Mediterranean*, N. Laneri (ed.), Chicago: Chicago Oriental Institute Publications, pp. 39–68.
Selz, 2011	Selz, G. J., "Remarks on the Empirical Foundation of Early Mesopotamia," in *The Empirical Dimension of Ancient Near Eastern Studies / Die empirische altorientalischer Forshungen*, G. J. Selz (ed.), Wiener Offene Orientalistik 6, Wien: Lit Verlag, pp. 49–70.
Sjöberg 1994	Sjöberg, A. W., "Abzu," in *Pennsylvania Sumerian Dictionary Project* A/II, pp. 185–202.
Spycket 1992a	Spycket, A., *Les figurines de Suse*,1. *Les figurines humaines IVe–IIe millénaires av. J.-C.*, Ville royale de Suse 6. Mémoires de la Délgation archéologique en Iran 52. Paris: Gabalda.
Spycket 1992b	Spycket, A., "Terracotta Figurines," in The Royal City of Susa: *Ancient Near Eastern Treasures in the Louvre*, P. O. Harper et al (eds.), New York: Harry N. Abrams, pp. 183–196.
Strouhal 1973	Strouhal, E., "Five Plastered Skulls from Pre-Pottery Neolithic B Jericho," *Paléorient* 1–2, pp. 231–247.
Teeter 2010	Teeter, E., *Baked Clay Figurines and Votive Beds from Medinet Habu*, Oriental Institute Publications 133, Chicago: Oriental Institute Publications.

Trani 2002 — Trani, G., *Dalla creta alla cretazione. L'argilla in arte terapia*, Roma: Artemide.

Tringham and Conkey 1998 — Tringham, R., Conkey, M., "Rethinking Figurines: A Critical View from Archaeology of Gimbutas, the 'Goddess' and Popular Culture," in *Ancient Goddesses. The Myths and the Evidence*, L. Goodison, C. Morris (eds.), London: British Museum Press, pp. 22–45.

Ucko 1962 — Ucko, P. J., "The Interpretation of Prehistoric Anthropomorphic Figurines," *Journal of the Royal Anthropological Institute of Great Britain and Ireland* 92 (1), pp. 38–54.

Ucko 1968 — Ucko, P. J., *Anthropomorphic Figurines of Predynastic Egypt and Neolithic Crete with Comparative Material from the Prehistoric Near East and Mainland Greece*, Royal Anthropological Institute Occasional Papers 24, London: A. Szmidla.

Ucko 1996 — Ucko, P. J., "Mother, are you there?" *Cambridge Archaeological Journal* 6, pp. 300–304.

van Buren 1930 — van Buren, E. D., *Clay Figurines of Babylonia and Assyria*, New Haven.

van Buren 1931 — van Buren, E. D., *Foundation Figurines and Offerings*, Berlin.

Walker and Dick 1999 — Walker, C., Dick, M. B., "The Induction of the Cult Image in Ancient Mesopotamia. The Mesopotamian Mīs Pî Ritual," in *Born in Heaven Made on Earth: The Creation of the Cult Image in the Ancient Near East*, M. B. Dick (ed.), Helsinki 1999, pp. 55–122.

Waraksa 2008 — Waraksa, E. A., "Female Figurines (Pharaonic period)," in *UCLA Encyclopedia of Egyptology* 1(1), Willeke Wendrich (ed.), Los Angeles, http://escholarship.org/uc/item/4dg0d57b

Waraksa 2009 — Waraksa, E. A., *Female Figurines from the Mut Precinct: Context and Ritual Function*. Orbis Biblicus et Orientalis 240, Fribourg: Academic Press; Goettingen: Vandenhoeck & Ruprecht.

Wiggerman 1986 — Wiggerman, F., *Babylonian Prophylactic Figures: The Ritual Texts*, Amsterdam: Free University Press.

Wiggerman 1992 — Wiggerman, F., *Mesopotamian Protective Spirits*, Groningen: Brill.

Winter 1994 — Winter, I. J., "Radiance as an Aesthetic Value in the Art of Mesopotamia (With some Indian Parallels)," in *Art: The Integral Vision: a Volume of Essays in Felicitation of Kapila Vatsyayan*, B. N. Saraswati et al (eds.), New Delhi: DK Print World, pp. 123–132.

Winter 1995 — Winter, I. J., "Aesthetics in Ancient Mesopotamian Art," in *Civilizations of the Ancient Near East*, J. M. Sasson (ed.), New York: Hendrickson Publishers, pp. 2569–2580.

Winter 2000a — Winter, I. J., "Opening the Eyes and Opening the Mouth; the Utility of Comparing Images in Worship in India and the Ancient Near East," in *Ethnography & Personhood: Notes from the Field*, M. W. Meister (ed.), Rawat: Rawat Publications, pp. 129–162.

Winter 2000b — Winter, I. J., "Babylonian Archaeologists of the(ir) Mesopotamian Past," in *First International Congress,* pp. 1785–1798.

Winter 2002 — Winter, I. J., "Defining 'aesthetics' for non–western studies: the case of ancient Mesopotamia," in *Art History, Aesthetics, Visual Studies,* Clark Studies in the Visual Arts, M. A. Holly, K. Moxey (eds.), New Haven and London: Sterling and Francine Clark Art Institute, pp. 3–28.

Winter 2003 — Winter, I. J., "'Surpassing Work:' Mastery of Materials and Value of Skilled Production in Ancient Sumer," in *Culture through Objects. Ancient Near Eastern Studies in Honor of P. R. S. Moorey*, T. Potts et al (eds.), Oxford: Griffith Institute, pp. 403–421.

Winter 2007 — Winter, I. J., "Representing Abundance: A Visual Dimension of the Agrarian State," in *Settlement and Society. Essays Dedicated to Robert McCormick Adams*, E. Stone (ed.), Los Angeles-Chicago: Cotsen Institute of Archaeology, pp. 117–142.

Wrede 1990 — Wrede, N., "Katalog der Terrakotten der archäologischen Oberflächenuntersuchung (Survey) des Stadtgebietes von Uruk," *Baghdader Mitteilungen* 21, pp. 215–301.

Wrede 1991   Wrede, N., "Terrakotten und Objekte aus gebrannten Ton," in *Uruk: Kampagne 35–37 (1982–1984): Die Archäologische Oberflächenuntersuchung*, U. Finkbeiner (ed.), Berlin: Verlag Philipp Von Zabern, pp. 151–177.

Wrede 2003   Wrede, N., *Uruk. Terrakotten* I. *Von der 'Ubaid– bis zur altbabilonischen Zeit*, Mainz am Rhein: Verlag Philipp Von Zabern.

Ziegler 1962   Ziegler, C., *Die Terrakotten von Warka*, Berlin: Mann.

MARCO RAMAZZOTTI
Sapienza Università di Roma
marco.ramazzotti@uniroma1.it

Association for Coroplastic Studies 2014

Officers
Jaimee Uhlenbrock, President
Stéphanie Huysecom-Haxhi, Vice-President
Theodora Kopestonsky, Secretary

Executive Board
Marina Albertocchi
Rebecca Ammerman
Adi Erlich
Antonella Pautasso

Book Review Editors
Ioannis Mylonopoulos
Maya Muratov
Michael Anthony Fowler, Assistant Book Review Editor

Newsletter Editors
Alexander Nagel, Nos. 1 to 3
Jaimee Uhlenbrock, Nos. 4 to 11

Webmaster
Christine Aubry

The Association for Coroplastic Studies (ACoST) grew out of the Coroplastic Studies Interest Group (CSIG). Originally organized in 2007 as an Interest Group of the Archaeological Institute of America, the CSIG took its name from the word *koroplastes,* which in Greek antiquity was the term used for a modeler of images in clay. In view of the broad international membership that comprised the CSIG by 2012 and its over 200 members it was decided to separate from the Archaeological Institute of America and become an independant entity. Elections for officers and an Executive Board were held in 2012 and, after considerable deliberation, the name Association for Coroplastic Studies (ACoST) was adopted. ACoST members have organized conference sessions, conferences, symposia, colloquia, and a summer school on coroplastic studies, all focusing on coroplastic research. Currently, in 2014, 250 members from 21 countries around the world are conducting research on archaeological, historical, sociological, medical, religious, technical, and/or art historical issues pertaining to sculptural objects in made in clay.

http://www.coroplasticstudies.org

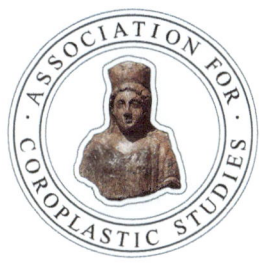

www.ingramcontent.com/pod-product-compliance
Lightning Source LLC
Chambersburg PA
CBHW050738180526
45159CB00003B/1265